◀ **Nacqueville** (the Hague peninsula) : *the 17th century castle and gatehouse, set in extensive grounds.*

Pour Thomas Sauoy, pour le remercier de ces belles vacances passées dans sa maison en Amérique.

Ségolène

Marie-Bénédicte Baranger
Lucien Bély

A Guide to Normandy

Translated by: Paul Williams
Angela Moyon

ouest
france

38, rue du Pré-Botté
35100 – Rennes

Bayeux : *Queen Matilda's tapestry. Harold is fatally wounded in the eye.*

◀ **Bayeux :** *the nave in the cathedral.*

ENGLISH
CHANNEL

NORMANDY

Armorican land mass
Clay
Silt deposits
Limestone

Seaside resort
summit

Map   B Thomazeau

INTRODUCTION

MEN FROM THE NORTH, NORTHMEN, NORMANS, INVADE THE COASTS

It was at the beginning of the IXth century that the first Northmen, Normans, or "men from the North" appeared in the Seine Bay and gave their name to this part of Gaul. It was already known the world over, and had reached as far as Russia. The Vikings, as they were known also, were above all made up of Danes and Norwegians.

*Were these sailors forced to leave their native land through poverty, and attracted by the wealth of more southerly territories ? Or was this vast migration of people due to the continuous violent efforts of the Carolingian kings, ever since Charlemagne, to extend Christianity and Latin civilisation as far as possible towards the east and the north ? Or were these simply a few adventurous, daring, restless, indomitable princes who abandoned the countries that no longer had room for them in order to become the fabulous, superhuman heroes of the **sagas**, the epic poems of the north ? These "sealords" were pagans in search of loot who launched more and more expeditions of a progressively bloody nature along the French coasts throughout the IXth century. Their remarkable ships, known as **drakkars** or **snekkars**, that were long, pointed, versatile, and swift, had dragons sculptured on the stern and the prow, and were able to stand up to the most terrible storms. The Bayeux Tapestry shows how these very beautiful ships were still very much in use two centuries later. On account of their shallow draught they could sail up rivers like the Seine. Every year the Normans pushed more deeply inland. Their hordes took terror wherever they went. Looting, rape, death.*

But these Vikings were not the first invaders. Bronze Age men had used the Seine valley as a route through to the magnificent Cassiterides islands, the kingdom of tin. The Celts of Gaul became established there. Their tribes left their names to Normandy : the Véliocasses to Vexin, and the Calètes to the district of Caux. Then there was the Roman occupation : three centuries of peace. An old theatre of Juliobona (or Lillebonne), or the ruins of a fort at

Château-Gaillard : *the fortress.* ▶

9

Jublains date back to that time. The Saxons came in vast numbers overturning the established order, and settled down firmly. Finally, the Franks came to impose their customs on the aristocracy : they established the authority of the diocese of Rouen and founded the first abbeys.

It was these monasteries that above all took the attention of the pagan Normans. Gold had been accumulated there over the course of the centuries and was used to beautify objects associated with worship. The pirates stole ciboriums and reliquaries that were easy to transport on their ships, and then they would burn all the monastery buildings. In order to escape death, the monks had to flee in the face of this permanent menace. Jumièges was abandonned to the wild beasts and birds of prey. The relics of the founder saints were taken far away towards the east and the south.

The Vikings were also peasants. They soon stopped their annual expeditions and tried to settle on this rich, fertile coast. Around the Seine estuary and Cotentin peninsula they took over enormous areas of land. Hadn't they thrown overboard the wooden beams from their old abandoned houses which, on being washed ashore, showed them where to build their new homes ? From that moment this land belonged to them and it became clear that Charlemagne's successors could do nothing to contain the Viking invasion. They had to compromise. Charles the Simple and a Viking chief by the name of Rolf le Marcheur (the Walker) came to a strange agreement known to history as the Saint-Clair-sur-Epte treaty. The king recognised the authority of the formidable warrior over this western province, and the Norman recognised the sovereignty, albeit completely theoretical, of the Frankish king. Rolf had to establish himself as the leader of this new "Normandy". He became a Christian, swore to defend his new faith and to force his people to adopt it, and to take over the "Roman" language. Rolf became Rollo, or Robert. The river Epte became the new frontier.

After much fighting, Rollo brought peace to this land that had up till then been given over to anarchy. Legend has it that he hung up some golden bracelets in a forest, being sure that they wouldn't be stolen, in order to show how strong were his law and justice. Many people from the north thronged towards Normandy. Christianity was a means of bringing them together even though the old gods of the woods and of the lakes continued, above all in the Cotentin region, to be foremost in people's minds. Thor's hammer seemed to offer just as much protection as the Christian cross. However, in Normandy as elsewhere, the general rule held good : the conquering invader came to adopt the civilisation — i.e. the language, faith and values — of the conquered that were already settled there.

DUKES AND KINGS FOR A POWERFUL NORMAN STATE

The Viking chief gradually took the title of "Duke" of Normandy. He would travel from town to town for, although since Rollo's time Rouen had been the obvious capital of the Duchy, there were many towns vying with each other for the privilege. At Bayeux whose governor Béranger was Rollo's father-in-law, William Long Sword was born. Richard II made Fécamp the spiritual centre of his kingdom and made it into a famous place of pilgrimage by establishing there the monastery of the Trinity. But, finally, it was Caen that William preferred, for his wife Mathilde lived and died there and they both made the town into a "Benedictine city". The prince was surrounded by a veritable court, and its brilliance attracted noble foreign visitors. Some great dignitaries, either ecclesiastical or lay, were given precise tasks. The Duke would make his relative into counts and send them as governors of territory on the frontiers. He would entrust to "viscounts", nominated by him and answerable only to him, the administration of his domain. In this way, vassals and loyal subjects exercised a system of mutual restraint. Norman law was respected everywhere : ducal justice and peace reigned. Power was based on a feudal hierarchy at the top of which without doubt was the Duke ; but in this society, serfdom, although common in Europe, did not exist for the men from the North knew nothing of it. Nevertheless, the Normans readily practised a slave trade, for the

Slavonic tribes were easy prey that suited perfectly the Arab Emirs from Spain. Thus a Norman state was built and its firm foundations were much admired by the whole of Christanity. Its power was in direct contrast with the disorder that was still abundant all over Europe. So powerful indeed was it that William could plan and successfully carry out the conquest of England where all he had to do was impose the political and social structure of his Duchy, much to the benefit of the Normans themselves.

Violence reigned in the west and princes died young leaving sons that were still children : in 942 at the death of his father William Long Sword, Richard I was ten years of age ; Robert took over the Duchy at the age of seventeen in 1027, and on his death in 1035 the bastard son William was only seven. In order to impose their authority on their rivals and vassals, these young children had to struggle for a long time, manœuvre between rival factions, prevent intrigue, fight on the frontiers. For this reason the king of France declared himself protector of the young Richard I and subsquently imprisoned him at Laon. Richard escaped and, with the help of pagan Vikings, defeated the French. He favoured one of the king's rivals, the Duke of France, Hugues le Grand, his father-in-law ; and finally he set up his brother-in-law Hugues Capet as king who founded a new and long-lasting dynasty. All the princes were cruel warriors and when, round about the year 1000, a peasant revolt broke out caused by anxiety and famine, Richard II's repression knew no bounds. Like their ancestors, they too loved adventure. Robert the Liberal, well before his son William, cherished the desire to conquer England, and he died in the end, exhausted and ill, while travelling in the Holy Land. Often, the Viking's descendants loved debauchery : once, on entering Falaise, Robert caught sight of Arlette, a tanner's daughter, washing clothes in the fountain. That very evening in the Duke's bed, this beautiful woman saw in a dream a tree emerging from her body and going right up towards heaven : she was to give birth in fact to little William, the future conqueror of the British Isles.

Under this king Normandy became the continental part of a vast island kingdom. Little by little the princes considered themselves to be more English than Norman, and yet they retained many of their ancestor's characteristics. Henry II is the best exemple of this. For twenty years this great-grandson of the Conqueror had to fight, aided by his supporters, in order to maintain his kingdom. His father, Geoffroy Plantagenêt, had added Anjou to the possessions of his wife, the Empress Mathilde. The hot-headed Eleanor d'Aquitaine, weary with her husband the king of France, went and offered Henry her immense principality : this was a marriage both of love and politics. Henry thus became the most powerful ruler in Christendom, and as mediator he could set up all manner of matrimonial ties throughout the Christian world through his sons and daughters. This ostentatious and debauched ruler depended on sound finances and a strong army. His subjects were devoted to him. But he was also cruel : he was the instigator of the "murder in the cathedral", when Thomas à Becket was killed at Canterbury in front of the altar by friends of the king who once was his friend. His decline from power came later when this proud monarch saw his sons turn against him, supported by Eleanor. With his old age that was so full of bitterness, the end of the Anglo-Norman Empire was near at hand.

FROM JUMIEGES TO LESSAY : THE SPLENDOURS OF THE ROMANESQUE AGE

For a long time historians described this development of Christian art in the west as "Norman", and this has now come to be known in the XXth century as "Romanesque" art. The abbeys were the richest examples of this : the XIth century, thanks to the peace and prosperity of the Duchy, was the age of full Benedictine maturity. Richard II established at Fécamp a demanding and ardent Abbot, William of Volpiano, who brought moral, intellectual and spiritual reform to all Norman monks. Henceforth, the princes and their vassals heaped gifts and lands upon them so that they should pray to God for them, the sinful laity, and so that their bodies on their demise could be buried in the shadow of the monasteries.

Saint-Martin-de-Boscherville : *arching round the main door of the abbey church of Saint-Georges-de-Boscherville.*

◄ **Domfront** : *the church of Our-Lady-on-the-Water.*

Richard II was the protector and benefactor of Mont Saint-Michel and his wife founded Bernay Abbey. The one at Fontenelle was restored and took the name of its VIIth century founder, the count of king Dagobert, saint Wandrille, the true "Athlete of God". As for William the Conqueror he founded at Caen the abbey of Saint-Etienne, later to be known as the "abbaye-aux-Hommes" (the Men's Abbey), and his wife Mathilde founded Trinity Abbey (the Women's Abbey). In this way they hoped to bribe the Church and the Papacy which condemned their marriage on account of their blood relationship. After the conquest of England, William asked men of the Church to govern his kingdom. In particular he summoned an erudite Italian, Lanfranc, who became Archbishop of Canterbury. This brilliant intellectual, after having taught at Avranches, had retired into the community founded by the knight Herluin or Hellouin. It was thanks to him that Bec-Hellouin Abbey had become the great intellectual centre of the western world.

Time took its toll of the abbeys, and today grandiose ruins testify to this great religious and architectural effort. Jumièges abbey was purchased during the Revolution by a wood merchant who wanted to use it as a source of stone. He had no hesitation in destroying the tall and elegant lantern-tower which towered above the transept. Fortunately one side of it was retained. This church better than any other brings together all the achievements of Norman architecture. The sense of the vertical and the quality of the light both triumph. The facade is

15

Symbols

⚲ Abbey

⚫ Priory

♜ Cathedral

▲ Collegiate church

Map B. Thomazeau

RELIGIOUS BUILDINGS

dominated by two high towers, and this harmony was imitated everywhere in Europe where the Normans made their presence felt, but particularly in England and in Sicily.

Extreme simplicity was the rule. The facade of Saint-Etienne at Caen symbolises the sobriety of this art where all is sacrificed to the purity of the architectural lines. Ornamentation is rare : there are no rose windows and no engraving on the stone. Such is the heritage of Ravenna handed down by Lanfranc. Bayeux cathedral that was finished by bishop Odo, half-brother of William the Conqueror, still has some traces of Romanesque decorative art : despite the transformations that took place in the Gothic age, the stone wall above the arches seems to have been plaited like hair ; and bas-reliefs on the corner-stones were no doubt inspired by Irish manuscripts where Asian influence was marked. The long nave is made to look longer by numerous bays supported by alternate pillars and columns, and it gains in height because of a long gallery topped by a clerestory. In order to lighten the general impression of the building the Romanesque architects rejected heavy stone vaults in favour of wooden beams.

Other naves have survived, sometimes mutilated, sometimes transformed like that of Mont Saint-Michel or that of Cerisy-la-Forêt which is reduced to three bays that are extremely high and divided into three storeys which are echoed in the chancel and the apse. In addition

16

to the great monasteries small establishments were scattered throughout the duchy wherever nobles wished to establish a group of monks. Hence Raoul de Tancarville founded Saint-Georges-de-Boscherville Abbey ; and Guillaume Paisnel, a member of a rich and powerful family of the Cotentin region, founded Hambye, where the absence of side-aisles contributes to the narrowness of the nave. Near a vast moor, the noblemen of La Haye-du-Puits erected at Lessay an abbey that was much loved by Barbey d'Aurevilly. The church was severely damaged in 1944. Now that it has been restored it is a model of Romanesque architecture on account of the sobriety and purity of its lines, the strength of its vaults and the soft beauty of the light that comes through its stained glass windows.

THE AGE OF THE CATHEDRALS

In 1204 Philippe-Auguste took over Normandy. The duchy became a French province that began to participate in the prosperity of the kingdom. The outstanding figure in this long XIIIth century was without any doubt this pious and just king, the arbitrator of all Europe, saint Louis IX. Political peace encouraged building and artistic research. The art form known as "Gothic" was born in Ile-de-France even though the sweep of the ogival arch, that allows for so much architectural daring, is of Anglo-Norman origin ; even though the facades are based on those of the great abbeys of the west. Norman art as such is but one aspect of French art.

This was the age of the cathedral. Since the cathedral was a town church that housed a bishop, it was a symbol of the new supremacy of the city over the countryside, of the bourgeois over the peasant, of the secular clergy over the monks. Rouen, Bayeux, Evreux, Coutances, Lisieux... These huge cathedrals sprang up from the remains of older buildings, that had suffered damage or been destroyed by fire. Often, as in the case of Coutances cathedral, the Romanesque towers were strengthened ("enveloped") so that they could sustain the tall spires, and cantoned with gracious turrets. Above the transept crossing was the lantern-tower : the octogonal one of Coutances, known as "the Lead" links the sweep of the vertical with the delicate mastery of the decoration.

Building work continued for many years. Rouen cathedral with its long nave, simple chancel that is delicate and graceful, and its stained glass windows, was finished at the end of the XIIIth century, but it was much changed over the course of the centuries. On its facade can be seen the different stages in its contruction : the Saint-Romain tower is an example of early Gothic ; the Saint-Jean door is in the decorative style of the XIIIth century ; but the exuberant Butter Tower and the Library were finished by Guillaume Pontis at the end of the XVth century.

Gothic art also gave to Normandy the "marvel" of the Mont Saint-Michel. To the north of the great abbey, vast, high-ceilinged rooms were built on three storeys to serve as a framework of the daily life of the monks. The rock, rising from the sand, gradually became a centre of pilgrimage in Normandy, and a symbol of the province. The poor were received in the Almonry which was next to the Cellar. Just above, noblemen were received by the Abbot in the bright room of the Guests. The clergy sought refuge next door in the "calefactory", now known as the "Knights' room". The floor above was reserved for prayer. The spacious Refectory looked out on to the cloister, suspended between heaven and earth. Here, small columns completely surround a little garden, and they in their turn are topped by sculptured corner stones and friezes in the soft white limestone of Caen. These leaves and fruit are one of the finest examples of decorative art in the Gothic age.

The end of the Middle Ages (which was an "autumn" of great beauty) saw Gothic art become technically brilliant and exceptionnally decorative : it became "flamboyant". One of the most successful examples of this art form is Saint-Ouen church in Rouen. There, everything is sacrificed to the majesty of the interior proportions, and to the delicate beauty of the

Saint-Wandrille : *the ruins of the abbey church.*

◄ **Rouen :** *13th century stained glass in Notre-Dame cathedral. Christ washing the disciples' feet, and the Last Supper* (detail).

*pierced gallery or **triforium**. And since the cardinal of Estouteville, abbot of Saint-Ouen, was also abbot of the Mont Saint-Michel, he ordered his architects to look to Rouen for inspiration when restoring the ruined chancel at Mont Saint-Michel. A chevet, resting on a veritable forest of granite, rises from the top of the rock. It is reached by the famous "Lace Stairway" which has such an evocative name. If Rouen is the capital of Flamboyant art in Normandy, its masterpieces are imitated throughout the province : Magdalene church in Verneuil-sur-Avre is based on Butter Tower, and at Caudebec is "the most beautiful chapel of the kingdom" according to king Henri IV. Despite all this a local form of statuary survived. At the beginning of the XIth century Enguerrand de Marigny had already given the sculptors of Ecouis the task of decorating the collegiate church. This tradition was upheld at the beginning of the XVIth century when statues were carved in like manner for Notre-Dame church at Verneuil.*

THE TEMPTATION OF ADVENTURE :
FROM NORMAN KINGDOMS TO GREAT DISCOVERIES

Was the Norman taste for adventure in fact a Scandinavian tradition ? In the XIth century some knights left their peaceful province to try their luck in far-off lands. At the time,

Christianity was spreading over the whole world : the Holy Land in Islamic hands, and the Byzantine Eastern Empire fascinated nobleman, pilgrim and adventurer alike. One family, descended from a small Cotentin baron called Tancrède d'Hauteville achieved fame during these illustrious times. The eldest of Tancrède's twelve sons, Guillaume, became duke of the Pouilles thanks to the violence and the warfare raging in Italy. Robert Guiscard, a younger son in the family, together with his descendants, managed to establish a Norman kingdom in Sicily. Their heir Manfred, the romantic hero acclaimed by Dante, Byron and Schumann, in 1265 fell at the hands of saint Louis's brother, Charles of Anjou. Bohémond of Sicily, one of Robert Guiscard's sons, was one of the leaders of the first crusade and managed to carve out for himself a principality around Antioch, a large town in the Middle-East. His descendants remained there for a long time through intermarriage with local rulers. These Mediterranean kingdoms are proof of the glory and power of the Norman barons.

At the end of the Middle Ages, it was the Atlantic Ocean that attracted the Normans. Thanks to progress achieved in navigation and science, Europe was discovering new continents. The Norman ports of Dieppe and Honfleur despatched their intrepid sailors all over the world. A "Petit Dieppe" was founded on the Guinea coast in 1364. In 1402 Jean de Béthencourt, a gentleman from the Caux District, became "king of the Canary Isles". So much for Africa. Two natives of Honfleur were among the first to visit the American continent. Paulmier de Gonneville reached Brazil in 1503, and Jean Denis visited the mouth of the Saint-Lawrence in 1506. At the beginning of the XVIth century, François 1st encouraged this spirit of discovery. In 1517, to replace Harfleur which was silting up, he created the "haven of grace", now known as Le Havre, where high tide lasts for two hours. The "maritime adviser" to the king, Jean Ango, armed a whole flotilla at Dieppe to attack ennemy ships. His beautiful manor house near Varangeville-sur-Mer is still in existence as a proof of his enormous fortune. The Floretine Verrazano, "principal pilot" of François, left from Dieppe to explore Nouvelle-Angoulême, the future New York. Then, in the wake of the Wars of Religion, came the great protestant attemps. Proud admiral Villegaignon tried to colonise Rio de Janeiro with Huguenots from Le Havre. His attempt failed in 1555. A similar attempt in Florida met the same unfortunate end. Success came later at the beginning of the XVIIth century : a privateer from Dieppe left Honfleur and founded Quebec in 1608. His name was Samuel Champlain and this was the birth of Canada. Throughout the XVIIth century the discovery of new lands fascinated the Normans. Cavelier de la Salle had been born at Rouen in the Rue du Gros-Horloge. Like so many others before and after him he wanted to discover the legendary North-West Passage to China. His haughty manner caused him to clash with missionaries in Canada. However, after the Great Lakes he reached the Mississipi and followed it to the gulf of Mexico. In homage to king Louis XIV he gave the land the fine name Louisiana. The proud adventurer died some years later at the hands of his own men.

Louis XIVth was too fond of war. He waged it as much at sea as on land. And he called on the Normans as sailors and admirals to man his fleets. A man from Dieppe, a certain Abraham Duquesne, of the reformed religion, was feared over all the seas of Europe. Tourville, a native of the Cherbourg Peninsula, fought under him. Off Barfleur on 29 May, 1692, with very inferior forces, he managed to contain and weaken a huge Anglo-Dutch armada. The victorious admiral began to withdraw but a terrible storm forced him to beach his ships at Saint-Vaast-la-Hougue. All the English had to do then was to set fire to them. To prevent such a disaster happening again, Vauban advised that a port should be built at Cherbourg on the tip of the Cotentin Peninsula. The work commenced as late as 1776 : the "Channel Inn" was being built. To stand up against the sea, ninety wooden cones filled with rubble and mortar, were sunk. This massive enterprise caused king Louis XVI to travel in great pomp across Normandy. This was his only big journey before his unfortunate flight to Varennes. One of these cones was positioned in the sea before the eyes of the monarch, but it was Napoleon III who, in 1858, finally inaugurated the military port. The Ocean had resisted man for three quarters of a century.

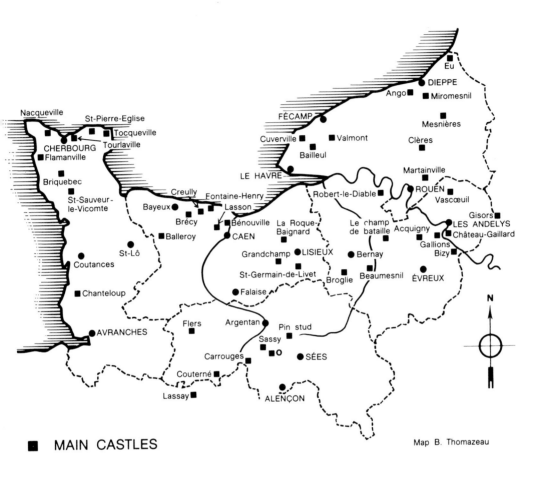

Map B. Thomazeau

■ MAIN CASTLES

NORMANDY ON THE VERGE OF EPIC HISTORY

    Three times in a thousand years the history of Normandy has been of epic proportions. The fate of Europe, nay of the entire world, was at stake.

    On September 27, 1066, William, Duke of Normandy, left the port of Dives, now near Cabourg. He was going to conquer England, and William was about to become the "Conqueror". This bastard son had had to fight the pagans of the Cotentin region, his ambitious relatives and his sovereign, the king of France, in order to get his way. The king of England was William's cousin but, on his death, it was his brother-in-law the Saxon Harold Godwinson who took the crown. Now formerly, this man, after having landed on the Picardy coast, had

21

Thaon : *the old church.*

◄ **Jumièges :** *Notre-Dame abbey church.*

submitted to the powerful Duke and under oath had recognised the latter's rights to the English throne. The vast, dangerous and costly expedition was to punish Harold who had been excommunicated by the Pope. The great battle of Hastings was not decisive but the Saxon had succombed. By October 1066 the Normans who had already established a powerful presence on English soil, settled down for good. The Bayeux tapestry tells this epic story. This large piece of embroidery was undertaken on the orders of Bishop Odo, William's half-brother. It is a masterpiece that contains humour, intelligence and poetry, a veritable Scandinavian saga, and it is the very first "cartoon strip". The Normans gave to England their language, laws, customs and art. A vast Norman kingdom henceforth stretched out on both sides of the Channel.

When Normandy became a French province during the XIIIth century, the English began to covet her. The second important date was July 12, 1346, when Edward III, king of England, landed at Saint-Vaast-la-Hougue on the tip of the Cherbourg Peninsula. A great Norman nobleman, Godefroy d'Harcourt, revolting against the king of France, guided him across the province. In this way the One Hundred Years' War began. The French cavalry suffered crushing defeats at Crécy, Poitiers, Agincourt. Armies, local conflicts, and also the plague raged across Normandy. And, for thirty years, the province became English. This was the time of the "Goddons", the nickname given to the English because of their swear word "God damn". Henri V, then his brother the regent, Duke of Bedford, imposed an adaptable, kindly rule which united noblemen, bishops, abbots and bourgeois. National feeling was sadly lacking during the XVth century. However, a young woman gave fresh impetus to it. She was the inspired shepherd girl from Lorraine known as Joan of Arc. But she was burnt on May 30, 1431, in Vieux-Marché square at Rouen.

The third crucial time for humanity was "D-Day", the "Longest Day", and this, on the coasts of Normandy, changed the destiny of the world. The Allied forces landed : the Americans at Omaha and Utah ; the English and Canadians at Gold, Juno and Sword. Man fought in conjunction with the aeroplane and the armoured division. Generals Montgomery, Eisenhower and Patton led the attack. On June 6, 1944, the great assault against Hitler's fortress commenced. Thanks to a turning movement the Cherbourg Peninsula was reconquered. Cherbourg fell in June. Meanwhile in the east, Caen began to yield after two months of fighting and eleven days of burning. Afterwards, the battle of Saint-Lô, the painful "hedge war" put the newly landed troops in danger, for the Normandy woodland with low-lying paths bordered by grassy banks made all progress difficult. Finally on July 25 "Operation Cobra" managed to break through. A German counter-offensive around Mortain was quickly stopped. Normandy was in Allied hands but the country was laid waste. Whole towns lay in ruins. At the end of the war it was necessary to rebuild. Caen became a town with a new face. The land round the castle was cleared and the building regained its former splendour. The name of Auguste Perret, the architect, was associated with the reconstruction of Le Havre. He was instrumental in the building of the modern city centre, the Porte Océane and Saint-Joseph's church. Many monuments had to be strengthened after being damaged, like the church of Saint-Maclou in Rouen whose beautiful doors were decorated during the Renaissance by Jean Goujon.

DEAUVILLE, TROUVILLE, CABOURG OR SEA-BATHING

Because of its proximity and its history, Normandy is too closely linked to England not to have adopted its customs. One has survived : sea-bathing, invented doubtlessly at the end of the XVIIIth century. Alexandre Dumas (the elder) may well have liked walking naked on Trouville beach, but it was the Duchess of Berry, the daugther-in-law of king Charles X, who first dared to bathe in public at Dieppe. It was, of course, for her health, for a white-gloved doctor escorted her into the sea. The immersion of Her Royal Highness was marked by the firing of a cannon. With the help of snobbery the medical pretext changed to one of pleasure. Water, sand and sun attracted people from now on to spend whole days on beaches. Such complete "leisure" in a life-style based on the sun, such farniente, played an important part in the lives of well-to-do families. They desired, organised, waited patiently for these "holidays". The aristocracy for a long time preferred to stay in their country castles and left

24

the seaside resorts to the rich bourgeoisie. But, with the Second Empire reconciliation between the classes was near at hand. The Duke of Morny, brother of Napoleon III, son of Queen Hortense and grandson of Talleyrand, shady financier, skilful politician and a spiritual person, made Deauville a rendez-vous for the Parisian smart set. The railway made access to the coast easier from the capital and, whilst leisure became adopted by all classes, "excursion trains" took towndwellers, desperate to get away, to the coast for the sacred **week-end**. Along the coast, summer residences, baroque and extravagant "villas" inspired by Italy, or traditional, comfortable and homely cottages began to be built.

A whole world was in the making : Marcel Proust, lover of "jeunes filles en fleur" was the entertaining, subjective muser that chronicled it all. Behind the imaginary Balbec is the very real and elegant Cabourg. The young man haunts the corridors of the Grand Hotel, that luxurious palace in the town. For a strange form of architecture developed in the seaside resorts. The sea front was privileged with its noble white façades, and, as at Deauville or Trouville, its "walks" along which people could saunter. Thus was born a society, made up of creatures of habit, lawyers, barristers, and the first president. It had its own customs, distractions and stories. During the day everyone took the sun. Unlikely-looking striped bathing costumes appeared but the ladies more often than not remained conservative in their appearance. Bathing machines on wheels were dragged into the sea whenever one of the ladies within decided to risk it. People lived "in the open air, before the waves" as Proust would have it, and this was a great innovation. But the quiet contemplation of the water was not sufficient to occupy the long evenings. So the holidaymakers strolled along the jetty and that was where little Marcel saw for the first time the lively and mischievous Albertine and her friends. When he was older, Marcel Proust went to the casino to gamble and dance. The casinos, that occupied imposing buildings in the resorts, often were the main attraction of the town, as in the case of Trouville and Deauville. To pass away the time, groups of friends paid visits : hence the "Verdurin clan" went to the "Patronne" on the outskirts of Balbec. Or they would visit as tourists this province and its churches which were being rediscovered at the end of the XIXth century. Finally, from across the Channel came sport, tennis and horse riding in particular, to attract the young. The sea now began to fire the imagination of painters. The elegant world of the sea-side resorts inspired Eugène Boudin. He attracted to Saint-Siméon farm at Honfleur, the founders of Impressionism.

The coast of Caux with the town of Etretat, the Norman cliffs with Honfleur, the Floral Coast with Deauville and the estuaries of the rivers Touques and Dives, the Calvados coast including Courseulles, the coast of the Cherbourg Peninsula with Granville, the whole Normandy coastline had found a new vocation : giving pleasure and leisure to man.

EMMA BOVARY : A ROMANESQUE TANG

Of course, Malherbe the poet was born in Caen, and Corneille the dramatist was born in Rouen. But Normandy is hardly present in their work. Alexis de Tocqueville, statesman and lucid historian of **The Ancien Régime and the Revolution** hardly evokes it either despite having lived for a long time in his parents' château on the tip of the Cherbourg Peninsula.

On the other hand, the novel is profoundly rooted in Normandy soil. Under the influence of the realist and naturalist schools, writers looked for new inspiration in provincial reality. Normandy with its countryside and its people offered a means of escape to the bourgeois, men of letters and the Parisians. Hence the imaginary place called Yonville-l'Abbaye was born with its silent, obstinate peasants and its self-centred, smug local dignitaries. Here, for eternity a young woman called Emma Bovary, Madame Bovary, dreams, becomes bored, loves and suffers.

Normandy is the favourite setting of the novels of Gustave Flaubert, this "family idiot" who was born in Rouen and lived at Croisset where he became the "hermit". **Bouvard and**

Fécamp : *screen in one of the chapels of Holy Trinity church.*

◄ **Carrouges :** *the castle gatehouse.*

*Pécuchet go there and carry out their insane experiments there. And it is at Pont-l'Evêque that Félicité, the "**simple heart**", humble servant of Madame Aubain, lives and dies. Was it not a stained glass window in Rouen cathedral which inspired Flaubert to write his **Legend of saint Julian Hospitaller** ? Maupassant, the spiritual son of Flaubert also tried to depict humble folk such as **Boule-de-Suif**, the Rouen prostitute, or the girls from the **Maison Tellier** at Fécamp. But for these men of letters the Normandy countryside was also a birth place, full of memories, and a retreat. The marquis of Maupassant was born in Miromesnil Château near Dieppe. He no doubt had this in mind when he depicted the Trembles' estate in **A life.** Barbey d'Aure-*

villy, the "leading man of letters", was born at Saint-Sauveur-le-Vicomte, near Hambye Abbey. The Cotentin region is always in his work with its heroic aristocrats like the **Chevalier des Touches**, its painful, nostalgic longings for Valognes in the shade of the beautiful Beaumont hotel, its disturbing peasant women like **The Woman Bewitched.**

Normandy is a main character in other novels. The countess of Ségur goes during the summer to depict her young, innocent **perfect little girls** against the backcloth of her château called Nouettes where she creates a reassuring and yet curiously deformed image of childhood and nature. In the **Aiguille creuse** of Etretat, Arsène Lupin, the gentleman burglar of Maurice Leblanc, accumulates his booty after his misdeeds and exploits. But the humorist Alphonse Allais, the son of the pharmacist in Honfleur, evokes the picturesque and provincial quality of the region ; Lucie Delarue-Madrus sees it as poetical ; and the philosopher Alain gives it an eternal quality in his **Propos d'un Normand.** Normandy has its own novelists and men of letters but it is also one of the most fertile producers of the novel and French literature in general.

For Normandy has seduced many writers that were born elsewhere. On writing **The Immoralist** André Gide thought about the sands of Algeria but on the other hand he was also concerned with the gentle beauty of La Roque : his grandfather had lived there as neighbour to Guizot, the Cabinet minister, who in the ancient Val-Richer abbey, composed his historical works and who imagined himself to be living the life of a true Norman. Gide was buried near his family in the hamlet of Cuverville, where he used often to go. Maurice Maeterlink, of Belgian origin, creator of Pelléas, lived in Saint-Wandrille Abbey well before the Benedictines returned. And the traveller stumbles across so many of the place names which fascinated Proust and which are scattered throughout his work : Froberville, Rivebelle, Cambremer. And one only has to think of the importance of Normandy in the work and life of Victor Hugo ! Charles Vacquerie and his young wife had gone on a boat trip on the Seine. The rich property of his bourgeois family looked down over the river : Villequier, near the estuary, on September 4, 1843. Then suddenly the drama. The young woman fell into the water and Charles died trying to save her. This occurence was reported in the newspapers the following day, and Victor Hugo, on a journey with his mistress, read one of the papers and learnt of the death of his daughter Léopoldine. The poet every year went back to Villequier cemetery where he could see "...the distant sails going down towards Harfleur".

Baron Hugo, a peer of France, but a republican at heart, left in exile after Louis-Napoleon Bonaparte's coup d'Etat. He chose the Channel Islands. For twenty years he lived on Jersey then on Guernsey. He looked at the sea. He also wrote and this English land saw the birth of his great epics.

FROM RICHARD WACE TO ANDRE SIEGRIED
THE NORMAN SENSE OF IDENTITY ?

"The Normans are not French people" wrote André Siegfried in 1913 in his **Political Tableau of West France.** Has there really existed over the course of time a "Norman sense of identity" ? A people had settled there from the north and had created an autonomous State in Normandy. They had their own bard, one Robert Wace, an inspired and aggressive canon from Bayeux who, in his **Roman de Rou** attacked France and the French with great virulence. Other chroniclers like Orderic Vital contented themselves with celebrating the exploits of the Dukes. When Normandy became French these memories lived on and some noblemen at the beginning of the XIVth century called for the retention of Norman traditions. Louis Xth (the Headstrong) granted the Norman Charter, the first of its kind in France, which confirmed the traditional rights of the Norman people, if not of the province of Normandy.

When Jean "the Good" had the counsellors of his son Charles, Duke of Normandy, executed before his very eyes, it was because he feared an alliance between his son and his ambitious cousin from Navarre, Charles "the Bad", who was powerful in the duchy. And if, on the death of Charles V, Rouen raised a hue and cry, this was simply an outburst of anger on the part of the bourgeois and the people against unpopular taxes and it was very much in keeping with all the disturbances that were breaking out at the same time in all the big cities of France. Of course, in the XVIth century wars ravished the province, but they were stirred up by religious and not political passions, as was the case throughout the land. Also, although the Duke of Longueville was the governor of Normandy and a very submissive husband, the fiery duchess, sister of the "Grand Condé" was not able to make the province take up arms against Mazarin in the Fronde rebellion. The beautiful lady rebel had to take refuge in England. And during the French Revolution peasants and bourgeois accepted revolutionary excesses but they never dared to go as far as rebelling against Paris. There was but one young girl who left Caen and went to Paris, and there murdered a journalist in his bath : Charlotte de Corday d'Armont was making Marat a martyr of the Revolution.

When regional culture gave way to national culture during the XIXth century, some people in the name of folklore, but also because they wanted to preserve tradition, tried to recapture the original savour. Arcisse de Caumont promoted this new cult dedicated to Normandy. Historians like Léopold Delisle and the count of Beaurepaire, archaeologists like Auguste Le Prévot and l'abbé Cochet, poets like Louis Beuve, became associated with this effort. In the XXth century Jean de la Varende, a gentleman farmer haunted by the past, described the legends and customs of Normandy.

Thus, little by little, the province was rediscovered. Medieval monuments were brought back to life. Romanticism had transformed the taste of men. Mont Saint-Michel stopped being a dark prison and travellers in the lower reaches of the Seine overlooked by imposing fortresses thought that they recognised the landscapes of the Rhine and of the **burgs** that Hugo had described. Then came **tourism** : from now on everyone could discover Normandy **through field and sandy shore** as Flaubert entitled one of his works.

THROUGH FIELD AND SANDY SHORE :
THE LAND AND THE LANDSCAPE OF NORMANDY

Normandy is an "ocean of green" according to Stendhal, or this "dish of raw sorrel" which set Flaubert's teeth on edge. This is the memory which the traveller retains linked with the impressions received from reading literature. This province is however a land of contrasts.

In its western part it forms part of the Armorican land mass whose primary rocks have been eroded for so long. The Cotentin region is a "small Brittany" where old legends and beliefs live on. The northern points of this "finistère" are the two promontories, the Nez-de-Jobourg near Hague cape, and to the east, Barfleur Point. The port of Cherbourg in this peninsula would correspond to Brest, and Granville to Lorient. In this old land mass the Val de Saire is a delightful region with a mild climate and wooded slopes. The Cotentin coastline, formerly jagged like that of Brittany, has now become been filled in and rendered less wild by sandbanks. The heathland, as at Lessay, is deserted. Sometimes however it takes on the form of a **polder,** as for example at Créances. Natural fertilizers (sea-weed, sea-sand, silt) have made it fertile. Spurs of granite can be seen along the coastline, and also rocky islets out at sea. There are reefs between the mainland and the Chausey islands. And it was on a rock sur-

Grandchamp (nr. Lisieux) : the 16th and 17th century castle combining classical architecture ▶ and Norman timber-framing.

rounded by water and sand that Mont Saint-Michel Abbey was founded a thousand years ago. It juts out above the immense bay that bears its name.

The primary land mass rises towards the south of the province. The river Orne through its meanderings has given rise to a delightful countryside that is now called the Switzerland of Normandy. Clécy stands at the centre of leisure activities and fishing, where the main sports are boating, climbing, hiking and horse-riding. And still further to the south, the highest points of West France are to be found in Normandy. One is in the middle of Ecouves Forest, the home of is mature trees, deer and hunting. The other is Mount Avaloirs : the river Sarthe has cut a deep valley in the granite covered with heather and, in conjunction with the Pail Cornice and the Misère Valley, has given the district its rather ambitious and suggestion name : the "Alps" of Maine.

Further inland is the bocage, woodland, that thrives in the mild, humid climat of the west. It owes its name to the old french bos or bosc, meaning wood, and the region that extends from the south of Cotentin to around Vire and Flers is normally called the Bocage of Normandy. The forests that used to cover the whole of Normandy were cut down in the latter part of the middle age. Slowly, in the XIIIth and XIVth centuries, charters began to give authority to peasants to enclose their fields. Grassland did not come to the fore until the XIXth century when farmers gave up cereals in order to concentrate on breeding stock. For ten months of the year the meadows produce tender grass. During the short winter the animals leave the hedged grasslands where they have been put out to graze, and they are fed on beet, hay or cabbage.

Normandy is also part of the Paris Basin. The English Channel is quite new in geological terms for it now flows between two vast basins that the sea previously had covered with sediment. Hence the wide gulf into which the Seine flows. When the Alps were being formed, the sedimentary strata began to undulate. The higher parts are the Perche hills in the south which form a natural boundary between Beauce, Armorica and Normandy. And, right in the north of the province next to Picardy, there is a deep clayey hollow in the middle of the limestone : it is known as the "buttonhole" of Bray. Rivers flow into it and converge at Forges-les-Eaux spa. This grazing land provides Paris with milk, cream and cottage cheese.

Woodland and forest cover the basin, and the three departments of Lower Normandy (Calvados, Orne and Manche) account for one tenth of cattle in France and produce a tenth of milk consumed. Bessin, around Bayeux, is a clayey district covered with a network of hedges. Isigny and its butter, famed for its quality since the XVIIth century, bears witness to the prosperity of dairy-farming in this area. The Auge district with the rivers Dives and Touques, contains everything that is pleasant in Normandy. Did not Delphine de Custine go there to Fervaques château and receive occasional visits from her gentle friend Chateaubriand ? The reputedly poor combination of clay and flint has harboured a perfect form of woodland. In this highly gastronomic region, cider and cream have pride of place. Already in the XIIIth century Pont-l'Evêque and Livarot had achieved fame with their cheeses. At the beginning of the XIXth century near Vimoutiers, a farmer's wife called Marie Harel invented another one : it used to be covered with a bluish skin which is now white. It took on the name of the village which is now known all over the world : Camembert.

But in the middle of this hedged country exceptions appear, and more and more frequently towards the east. The quality of the soil, the climate, or local tradition can account for these patches of wide fields where few trees grow. They are known as "campagnes" and are around Caen, Argentan and Alençon in the west, and Neubourg and Evreux in the east. At times, whenever clay is present to enrich the soil, agriculture, dominated by cereals, can take

Bénouville : the castle.

place. Agriculture prevails north of the Seine, on the chalky plateau in the district of Caux. Sugar beet and flax are grown there. But there are some woods growing on the clay and flint sides of the valleys.

In the heart of Normandy, the Seine valley is a world unto itself. Over the ages, as the sea level was changing, the river cut deep. Cliffs, that get steadily higher, dominate the river as it flows towards its mouth. On the edge of one of them Richard Lion Heart built the formidable stronghold Château-Gaillard. Communication used to be difficult here for roads could not cross the deep valley and had to follow the plateaux. Two large bridges span the river at Tancarville and Brotonne, and they are both marvels of modern art and engineering skill. The river meanders widely and towns shelter where river crossings were easiest : Rouen, Duclair, Caudebec. As for the ports in the estuary, they were replaced as they became silted up or as ships got larger, and other ports were built further out : Lillebonne in Gallo-Roman times, Harfleur, Honfleur, then Le Havre in modern times. The river has changed course leaving behind it marshland such as Vernier Marsh. There were also many islands, marshes and sandbanks but a channel was gradually opened up. Along the river banks, extensive forests have been saved from destruction despite the fertile soil which would have been suitable for other purposes. Much appreciated by the knights of Clovis, the forests of Roumare, Mauny, Jumièges, the Trait and Brotonne were protected by later generations who were inveterate hunters.

Towering cliffs form the Channel coastline. Beyond Houlgate, dark rocks have been worn down by rivers ; this is the charmingly unusual site know as the "Black cows". In the Caux region, chalk provides a barrier against the sea. But it is a soft rock which, in places, has been sculpted by the waves. The finest examples are to be seen in Etretat (the Needle and the Downstream Gateway). The "valleuses" or clefts in the rock are high above the water, reminders of swift-flowing rivers which have long since disappeared. The villages of the Caux are often to be found nestling in these valleys. Harbours are few in number. To the west of the Seine, only Port-en-Bessin has facilities for modern trawlers. Honfleur and its Old Basin are now used by sailing enthusiasts. To the east of the Seine Estuary, lies Fécamp which has maintained the traditions of the Newfoundland fishermen who suffer, with their boats, the rigours of cod-fishing. Elsewhere, in Dieppe or Le Havre, the ports handle commercial traffic.

THE APPLE, COW AND THE HORSE

The apple is traditionally associated with Normandy. The Honfleur poetess Lucie Delarue-Mardrus loved evoking her childhood in Normandy whose "scent was in an apple". The nobleman of Gouberville who left behind him a veritable journal, "the book of reason", already had in the XVIth century in his Cotentin orchard twenty nine varieties of apple tree. Such trees are grouped around houses but at the beginning of May the whole countryside becomes covered in a layer of "blushing flowers" with "white satin trains" as Marcel Proust described them. Red apples, yellow apples, early varieties both tender and sweet from the Bocage district, later varieties that are firm and long-lasting from the Auge district : they are all "shaken" off the trees from September to December. Heaps of apples are piled up near the farms where they are to be used to make cider. What formerly used to be a medecine for many ills has in our day become a simple pleasure. A brandy called "Calvados" is made and is drunk between dishes at big dinner parties thus keeping up the old Norman custom. "On the corner of the table there were carafes of brandy" : a detail from Emma Bovary's wedding.

The selection of different breeds of cattle became a passion among farmers from the middle of the XIXth century. Emigrant noblemen who had come back to France wanted to copy English gentleman farmers. A Norman herdbook was brought into being to carry the names of the best breeding animals in the region. The English Durham breed had a wide following, but in the end the native Cotentin breed emerged as the best, and the Noël dynasty of breeders created a whole line of powerful bulls the most famous of which was Silencieux. This breeding turned into a highly speculative activity in Normandy agricultural circles. In an area which was becoming increasingly wealthy, and which lay so near Paris, it was evident that milk and meat consumption would encourage the expansion of this type of farming. One of the biggest cattle markets in France is held in Lessay on the west of the Cherbourg Peninsula in September.

Horse breeding stems from an old aristocratic tradition, for horses have always been the privilege of the aristocracy. Colbert created the Pin stud farm in Argentan, the main building of which was designed by Mansart. The finest breeds of stallion are raised there. The English thoroughbred was preferred from the XVIIIth century and this beautiful animal became the favourite for racing. At the end of August in Deauville the **yearlings** sale takes place and it is a business and social occasion. In 1937 horse breeding was enriched by a new thoroughbred, the French, or rather Norman trotter. For a long time agriculture had been using strong draught horses like the cob and above all the "percheron". The district of Perche with its wooded hills, fortified farms and lush meadows gave its name to this beautiful animal with a dappled coat, and its pedigree is very strictly controlled by the Société Hippique Percheronne.

MANOR HOUSES AND HOVELS

The archbishop of Rouen, cardinal Georges d'Amboise whose tomb adorns the cathedral, was the first to decorate his château at Gaillon in the Italian style. Thanks to him the Renaissance came to Normandy at the beginning of the XVIth century. It embellished unfinished churches and the chevet of Saint-Pierre at Caen, whose worked pinnacles and sculptured balustrades bear witness to the new style. It made public buildings under construction at the time more magnificent. This happened at Rouen with the palace that was to house the Exchequer of Normandy, then the Parliament instituted by François 1st, and finally, before the disaster of 1944, the Palais de Justice. But in a changing world this refined Italian art suited the rich and the aristocracy better than men of the Church and statesmen. It was used a lot on private architecture. Fortified châteaux became beautiful manor houses ; parks and gardens replaced moats and ramparts ; decorative windows replaced loop-holes. So a new life style took over in the châteaux of O and Fontaine-Henry. It also gained a hold in the towns where town houses like the Bourgtheroulde in Rouen or the Escoville in Caen remind one of this style which is sometimes associated with the last stages of the Flamboyant style. So the nobility over the centuries built manor houses right across Normandy : Carrouges in the XVIth century for the Le Veneur de Tillières family ; Balleroy for the descendants of Jean de Choisy in the XVIIth century and Bénouville, which was the work of Nicholas Ledoux, in the XVIIIth century. The Age of Enlightenment also saw changes in religious art. The monks wanted to change their life style. One of them, Guillaume de la Tremblaye, an architect and a sculptor, built new monastery buildings for the Abbaye-aux-Hommes at Caen, which he decorated with admirable wainscoting, and also for Bec-Hellouin.

The influence of different cultures linked to the availability of natural resources, has gone towards creating typical rural homesteads, the more accomplished of which are undoubtedly the "masures" or "hovels", scarcely an apt description of the opulent farmhouses of the Caux Region. Those in Auge, however, are know as "clos". A vast apple orchard is surrounded by embankments of earth planted out with elm trees, which Stendhal compared to "dikes". The house, byre, stables and dairy all lie within this enclosure. The large pond where cattle could go to water has often been replaced in our time by a water tower. A great gate shuts off this isolated, lush oasis from the outside world. The thatched roofs and the timber-

Montfarville (nr. Barfleur) : *the interior of the 18th century church, decorated c. 1880 by a* ▶ *local artist, G. Fouace.*

frame walls (made by inserting bricks or plaster into the spaces between supporting beams) are a very typical sight in Normandy.

Some have tried to establish a Scandinavian influence behind the organisation of these farms. The independant and authoritative chief would live in the centre of his fortified property. Around him were his servants, peasants and vassals. So there may well be a link across the centuries between the countryside of Normandy and the impressions of a far-off rural civilisation.

LAND AND SEA

The rich, fertile soil has given this province its innate knack of avoiding much bloody revolution and tragic misery. The calm and religious peasants have made this country-side what it is to the background rhythm of the seasons. Was it not Jean-François Millet, native of Cotentin, a farm hand turned painter, who immortalised the simple, daily movements of the labourers ? And in Giverny, a village in Vexin, Claude Monet, at the end of his life, continued capturing the same exciting moment on the canvas by replacing the grandiose outlines of Rouen Cathedral in broad daylight, with simple white water-lilies. This prudent and yet sensual change symbolises Normandy very well. In like manner, medieval artists and their noble patrons were able to offer up to God churches, abbeys and cathedrals : art was being born by rooting itself in time and space.

On the other hand, adventure came from the sea to engross a whole people, and some individuals in particular, in travelling to the end of the world, or to the banks of the Thames. The Normans arrived by sea ; William left to conquer England by sea. For this province, with all its seafaring traditions, looks out over the deep towards the west and the north.

These two worlds, that of the sailors, soldiers and explorers, and that of the peasants, bourgeois and artists, for a long time turned their backs on each other. But Normandy has always had this interior struggle to decide whether or not to accept the attraction of sea or land, to look inwards or outwards, to stay put or travel abroad. And her history shows her to be resourceful enough to manage all these things.

The introduction to this guide-book was written by Lucien Bély and translated by Paul Williams. The alphabetical list of towns, historical monuments and places of interest was compiled by Marie-Bénédicte Baranger and translated by Angela Moyon.

AIGLE (L') (Orne)
20 miles N.E. of Mortagne-au-Perche.

L'Aigle, which is the centre of the traditional metalworking industry of the Risle Valley, is the largest town in the Ouche Region.

Saint-Martin's church (église Saint-Martin), with its three aisles, spans several centuries from the Romanesque period to the Renaissance. There is a marked architectural contrast between the 12th century limestone* clocktower and Saint-Martin's tower which was built at the end of the 15th century in the very ornate Flamboyant style on the instructions of Arthur Fillon, the priest of Madeleine church in Verneuil-sur-Avre. Several of the statues inside the church have been sculpted by contemporary artists, and some of the stained glass is also recent.

The outbuildings of the **castle** house the "June 44" Sound and Waxworks **Museum** which relates the main phases of the Normandy Campaign. The castle itself was built by Mansart in 1690 on the site of a former fortress. It was restored after the bombing raids of the last war.

A few miles outside L'Aigle lies **Les Nouettes Castle** which supplied the Countess de Ségur with the setting for many of the "whimsical tales" she wrote for her grandchildren. The capriciousness and extravagant fancies of her heroine, Sophie, and the angry outbursts of Old Mother MacMiche were a far more effective way of teaching right and wrong than any straight lecture ! The castle is now a Centre for Maladjusted Children.

One of the most flourishing religious communities in the area, the **Abbey of St-Evroult-Our-Lady-of-the-Woods** (Saint-Evroult-Notre-Dame-des-Bois), was built on land between the sources of the rivers Risle and Charentonne. In 593, King Childebert and his queen came to visit St Evroult in his hermitage and ordered the building of a convent and basilica which was later destroyed by the Norsemen. After the reconstruction of the abbey in the 11th century, it became so prosperous that the building were again razed to the ground, this time to make way for a Gothic edifice surrounded by fortifications. However, these later buildings began to fall into disrepair at the end of the 15th century, and a large-scale restoration project has been necessary to save the surviving ruins.

The monument facing the 13th century vaulted porch commemorates the historian and chronicler Brother Ordéric Vital, who pioneered historical accuracy in his "Ecclesiastical History" which is written in Latin. He was also a keen supporter of the solitary austere type of monastic life (he founded the **Savigny Abbey** in wooded countryside near Mortain). In the museum, there are various exhibits from the Abbey. The well-known novel by La Varende, "Nez de Cuir", was set in this community.

Terms marked with an asterisk are listed in a glossary at the end of the book.

Grestain (nr. Honfleur) : *the Benedictine abbey in which Arlette of Normandy (mother of William the Conqueror) was buried, with her husband and son.*

◀ **Lassays** : *towers and nalls of the castle.*

On the borders of the Ouche and Perche Regions, in an area of woodland and pasture dotted with ponds and small lakes, lies the **Grande-Trappe Abbey** (near Soligny) which belongs to the Reformed Cistercian Order. The monastic traditions have been strictly upheld since the Abbey was founded in 1140 by the monks of Breuil-Benoît. At the end of the 17th century, the community was governed by the irascible Abbot de Rancé (nicknamed Abbot Tempest). He had retired from society on the death of his mistress, the Duchess of Monbazon (he was deeply moved when he saw her decapitated body prior to the funeral). His rule was rigorous and austere ; he introduced the vow of 'strict observance' which was soon to be commonplace throughout France. Chateaubriand wrote a "Life of Rancé" in 1844 as a penance prescribed for him by his confessor. It was to be his last book.

ALENÇON (Orne)
30 miles N. of Le Mans.

By its geographical position at the confluence of the rivers Sarthe and Briante, Alençon is the point of convergence of four regions : the Ile-de-France, Normandy, Brittany and the Loire Valley. The fortified village of Gallo-Roman times became part of the Duchy of Normandy at the end of the 10th century and its castle was handed over to the lords of Bellême.

41

Once it had been reunited with the Crown of France under Philippe Auguste, the County of Alençon was attributed several times to the younger sons of the Royal Family. It became a Duchy and Peerage and was particularly prosperous under the Duchesses of Alençon. The court of Margaret of Navarre, the sister of King François I, was one of the most brilliant in its day and it was there that the poet Clément Marot gained fame and fortune. At the end of the 17th century, Elizabeth of Orleans, Duchess of Guise, brought a new period of prosperity to the town.

It was in about 1650 that Madame La Perrière created a new type of lacework based on the Venice point which was then at the height of fashion. This "Alençon lace" was later produced by the Royal Factory established by Colbert in 1665, and then by local lacemakers. The delicate needlework ensured that Alençon's fame spread far beyond the frontiers of France, and today the School of Lacemaking is keeping up tradition. Its pupils still produce the minute bridles and "colbertines" which were so highly prized in days gone by, and their skill equals that of their predecessors.

Thérèse Martin (later Sister Thérèse of the Child Jesus) was born in Alençon in 1873 and she spent her childhood in the town.

Alençon was very badly damaged by the air raids that accompanied its liberation on 12th August 1944. Today, the county town of Orne is still a bustling shopping centre and, in addition, it boasts the main offices and factory of the Moulinex domestic appliance company. The rich surrounding countryside is given over to agriculture and the breeding of race-horses.

The **Church of Our Lady** (église Notre-Dame), built in the Flamboyant style of the 14th and 15th centuries, is noted for its richly-decorated early 16th century porch. In the series of sculptures representing the Transfiguration of Christ, St John is seen from back view ; legend has it that the apostle turned round in horror during the Wars of Religion.

All that remains of the **castle** built between 1385 and 1415 by the first Duke of Alençon, John I, is one gate flanked by two massive towers which today form the entrance to the prison, and the "Crowned Tower" which can be seen inside the walls.

The new **Museum of Fine Arts and Lacemaking** was opened in 1981 to house the collections which had, until then, been on show in the Town Hall and the **Ozé House**, a mediaeval residence.

To the south-east of the town lie the wooded slopes of the **Perseigne Forest.**

ALPS OF MAINE

On the borders of the counties of Orne and Mayenne lies the 1,368 ft Mount Les Avaloirs, which is the same height as the Signal d'Ecouves. These two peaks are the highest in north-western France. The range is some 75 miles long and forms the dividing line between the Normandy and Maine woodland regions.

The narrow valley of the Sarthe river cuts across wild countryside blanketed with heather and trees, and runs down to the village of **St-Cénéri-le-Gérie,** which has a Romanesque church.

To the south of the village of **St-Léonard-des-Bois** which, like St Cénéri, is built on a bend of the river, a picturesque drive leads to the valley of the Misère river, a tributary of the R. Sarthe.

Overlooking the whole region is the **Pail Ridge** (Corniche du Pail) which skirts the Alps to the west.

ANDELLE (VALLEY OF THE)

The river rises near the spa town of Forges-les-Eaux. Upstream, the R. Andelle provides irrigation for agricultural land, whereas its lower reaches run through a highly-industrialised area. Its tributaries, the Héron and Crevon, wind their way through the gentle slopes bordering the Lyons Forest.

Fontaine-Guérard Abbey was built on the banks of the river at the end of the 12th century by Robert the White-Handed, Count of Leicester, in a wooded setting near the rushing spring which has given the Abbey its name. Its founders set themselves the specific tasks of putting the water to good use and acquiring mastery over nature.

As early as 1219, the nuns adhered to the Cistercian Order. Indeed the unity of the ogival Gothic style of architecture reflects the austere layout of a Cistercian house. (The Order declared that all buildings should lead off the cloisters.) Characteristically, the end wall of the abbey **church** is formed by a flat chevet pierced by windows. The vaulting of the apse is still visible today. Although the cloisters no longer exist, one can still see the **Chapter House.** It is a finely-decorated elegant building with three aisles separated by slender columns. Two other rooms are also still in existence : the calefactory, a vaulted room similar to the Knights' Hall on the Mont St Michel, and the **dormitory** on the upper storey, a room with narrow windows and a vaulted ceiling of wooden trusses.

The 15th century **St Michael's Chapel** (chapelle Saint-Michel) was built on the site of the Cellarer's Office in memory of Sister Marie de Ferrières. She entered the convent to escape her husband's brutality and was murdered there.

The choir stalls have been transferred to the **Pont-Saint-Pierre** church, which also has carvings from the reign of Henri II.

At the confluence of the rivers Seine and Andelle, near the Seine's confluence with the R. Eure, there is a fine view over the three river valleys from a promontory with a name that conjures up a well-known legend : **Lovers'Hill** (Côte des Deux Amants). It is said that the king of the Pistreians had promised to give his daughter, Calixte, in marriage to any man who could run up to the top of the hill with her in his arms. Raoul reached the top of the steep slope (without the aid of the invigorating potion he had in his possession but refused to take) where he collapsed and died of exhaustion. When his loved one saw that he had died, she too passed away.

ANDELYS (LES) (Eure)
22 miles N.E. of Evreux.

Situated at the gateway to Normandy, the villages of Les Andelys are remarkable not only for the oustanding natural beauty of their setting on the banks of the R. Seine at the foot of tall chalk cliffs backed by hills and woodland, but also for their rich historical heritage.

On 6th March 1204, the last bastion of the Dukes of Normandy, **Château-Gaillard,** fell to the King of France.

Richard the Lionheart, King of England, had hastily constructed the imposing fortress in 1196 (he is reported to have said, "Ah ! my one-year-old daughter ! Isn't she beautiful ?") to prevent Philippe Auguste from reaching Rouen which had been under English rule for nigh on three centuries. The castle, overlooking a meander of the R. Seine, was a combination of all that was best in 12th century military architecture, based on the oriental systems of defence that the Crusaders had seen in the Holy Land.

On the death of King Richard, he was succeeded by his brother, John Lackland, and Philippe Auguste promptly declared that he would take the "Lion's Den". At the end of 1203, he isolated the castle from the surrounding countryside by having a deep ditch dug round it and placing wooden towers at regular intervals as an extra offensive measure. The ensuing siege lasted for six months but the inhabitants of the fortress still had food left. In view of the fai-

Balleroy : *the castle.*▶

lure of his plan to reduce the castle by famine, he attacked. In spite of the heroic fight put up by Constable de Lascy, the castle fell into the hands of the French king. One of his soldiers had managed to get in by way of the latrines, and had lowered the drawbridge. Three months later, Rouen had also been taken.

In 1314, Louis X the Headstrong had his wife, Margaret of Burgundy, imprisoned in Château-Gaillard with his sisters-in-law Jeanne and Blanche. All three were accused of adultery. Margaret was strangled in her cell two years later, as a punishment for the crimes committed in the Nesle Town House in Paris.

During the One Hundred Years' War, and the Wars of Religion, the castle suffered a series of misfortunes. It was partially demolished in 1603 by King Henri IV who gifted the stones to the Cardinal de Bourbon for his castle at Gaillon. The keep had already been razed to the ground on the orders of King François I.

The layout of the castle had made clever use of the terrain. The **outer bailey**, a triangular forework defended by five towers of which only the highest is still standing, protected the narrow strip of land connecting the citadel to the surrounding hills on the north side, and was separated from the main fort by an esplanade or **low defence.** Two concentric enclosures linked by two bridges were dominated by a cylidrical **keep** reinforced by piers. Projectiles thrown from the parapet would ricochet off the convolved base of the walls and cover distances that were otherwise unattainable. The keep was originally three storeys high ; its walls were 16 ft thick. The **Governor's House** is still in evidence, as are the **casemates** dug into the rock itself where the garrison kept its food. There is a particularly fine view of le Petit Andely from these casemates.

The village of **Le Petit Andely** on the right bank of a sweeping curve of the river, was fortified by Richard the Lionheart to serve as a look-out post on the frontiers of the Duchy not long before he ordered the construction of Château-Gaillard itself.

Further downstream is **Le Grand Andely,** birthplace of the painter Nicolas Poussin. The village grew up round a monastery founded in 511 by Queen Clotilde, the widow of Clovis. The collegiate church now stands on the site. Legend has it that the Queen encouraged the workmen by changing the water of the fountain (which still exists) into wine.

The **collegiate church of Our Lady** (Notre-Dame), which was founded in the 13th century, was altered and enlarged several times. The north and south sides are in contrasting styles, the former being Renaissance while the latter is Flamboyant. In the 13th century nave, a series of Renaissance stained glass illustrates scenes from the Bible. The very ornate organ loft dates from the same period. Haut- and bas-reliefs, wood carvings and sculptures in stone complete the decoration of the church, which also houses paintings by Poussin's teacher, Quentin Varin.

ARGENTAN (Orne)
28 miles N.W. of Alençon.

The town of Argentan is situated in an area of woodland where the principal occupation is animal husbandry. The lacework for which the town is famous rivals that of Alençon ('Argentan' lace is produced nowadays by the nuns of Notre-Dame Abbey). The town was plundered several times over the centuries, and was very badly damaged during the Liberation. However, there is still some evidence of its history.

Construction work on **St Germain's church** (église Saint-Germain) began in the 15th century but was not finished until 1641. Flamboyant Gothic and Renaissance architecture (e.g. the porch onto the Rue Saint-Martin) exist side by side or, occasionally, are combined as in the bell-tower and triforium*. At the far end of the chancel, there is an unusual four-sided apse with a double ambulatory and vaulted roof with pendants.

St Martin's church, like St Germain's, is undergoing restoration work at present. The stained glass in the chancel dates back to the Renaissance period.

The final offensives in the Battle of Normandy (1944) took place in the **Argentan Region,** at **Ecouché** on the R. Orne and **Chambois** in the Dives Valley where the Allied Armies joined up with each other.

Both Fernand Léger, the painter, and the poet Vincent Muselli were born in Argentan.

AUGE (REGION OF)

This is the wooded hinterland of the Floral Coast, stretching as far as the county of Orne. It is an agricultural area, dotted with manor-houses, and renowned for its poultry and its Calvados, or apple-jack — a vital part of any really substantial meal. It should be drunk in the middle to "make room" for the remaining courses ! The area is also well-known for its cider (especially the Cambremer vintage cider). Although produced in monasteries as far back as the 12th century, it did not become a commonplace drink until the 14th century after the Kings of Navarre had imported it into Normandy. However, the Auge Region owes its international fame not to its alcohol but to its dairy produce.

In the busy little town of **Vimoutiers,** hemmed in by hills on all sides, a statue of Marie Harel pays homage to the farmer's wife from the neighbouring village of **Camembert** who perfected the recipe for the famous cheese at the beginning of the 19th century. It is said that the secret had been passed on to her mother by a non-juring priest to whom she had given shelter during the French Revolution.

The soft ripened cheeses of **Livarot** and Pont-l'Evêque further to the north (q.v.) are a must for any gourmet's cheeseboard.

Surrounded by a vast moat filled by the waters of the R. Touques, **Fervaques Castle,** a brick and stone edifice dating back to the 16th and 17th centuries, perpetuates the memory of Delphine de Custine, Chateaubriand's much-loved lady friend. She bought the castle in 1803 and the writer paid several visits there during their somewhat stormy relationship.

Orbec has some fine old houses. It lies in the valley of the R. Orbiquet.

In the north-west of the region, **Auge Hill** (Côte d'Auge) provides the visitor with a variety of panoramic views, especially from **Clermont-en-Auge.** Here the view extends as far as the countryside round Caen.

AVRANCHES (Manche)
16 miles S.W. of Granville.

Situated near the Bay of the Mont St Michel, the town of Avranches, which was a bishopric from 511 A.D. to the French Revolution, played a part in the founding of the Mont. It was here that the archangel Michael appeared to Bishop Aubert in 708 and ordered him to build a sanctuary (cf. Mont Saint-Michel). Apart from several examples of antique gold plate, the **Church of St Gervais and St Protais** also possesses a reliquary containing the skull of the disbelieving bishop which carries the imprint of St Michael's finger.

Here, too, King Henry II, the Plantagenet monarch who had instigated the murder of Thomas à Becket in Canterbury in 1170, had to make amends for his crime in public outside the cathedral (which has since been destroyed). The paving stone on which he knelt in humble penance can still be seen today.

In 1639, when dislike of the governement because of excessive taxation turned to open revolt (known as the Barefoot Rebellion), the rebels murdered one of the King's agents in Avranches and set up their headquaters in the town.

Bayeux : *Queen Matilda's Tapestry. William the Conqueror and his fleet crossing the Chan-* ▶ *nel.*

38.

TRAN SIVI

ET VENIT AD

The last unsettled period was that of the Normandy Landings. The American Forces fought their way to a decisive but bloody victory in the campaign known as the 'Drive to Avranches'. A monument to General Patton was erected on a square which is now officially recognised as American territory.

The lexicographer Littré was born in Avranches, and Maupassant gave a famous description of the town in his novel "Notre Cœur".

From the terrace of the tastefully-landscaped **Public Park** (Jardin des Plantes), part of the grounds of a former Capucin Friary, there is a unique view across the Bay to the Mont St Michel and beyond, which can also be seen from the observation platform. Visitors may even fly over the island from the local airport.

The **Regional Museum-Library of Avranches** houses two hundred and three very rare manuscripts dating from the 8th to the 15th century. They originally belonged to the Abbey of the Mont St Michel. The renown of the Mont's library was far-reaching and although these manuscripts represent only a very small part of its total stock, the quality of their texts and their illuminations provide an invaluable reminder of the philosophy and culture of a bygone era. In particular, the manuscripts include extracts from the orations of Cicero, an original translation of Aristotle, Abélard's "Sic et Non", the Abbey's records, and the "Chronicles" by Robert de Torigi which are in fact the first-ever history of the Mont.

To the south of Avranches, the **Sélune Dams** (barrages de la Sélune), which were constructed at the beginning of this century across the narrow river of the same name, have created a string of manmade lakes.

BAGNOLES-DE-L'ORNE (Orne)
30 miles N.W. of Alençon.

Situated on the valley floor of the R. Vée in wooded countryside, Bagnoles-de-l'Orne and the neighbouring borough of Tessé-la-Madeleine are important spa towns specialising in the treatment of poor blood circulation and disorders of the endocrinal glands.

Hugues, the Lord of Tessé, had abandoned his faithful steed in the Forest of Andaine. The horse was old and sick, and Hugues could not bear to watch it slowly dying. A month later, to his astonishment, the horse came back frisky and full of life. Hugues noticed that it went regularly to bathe in a fountain where the water was warm. He submersed himself in the water and regained his own youth and strength.

This is the legend behind the discovery of the healing properties of the only warm spring in the west of France. The water has a temperature of 27°C. (81°F.) ; it has a very low mineral content but is highly radioactive. Since becoming famous in the 17th century, the Pump Rooms set amidst steeply-sloping gardens have catered for many well-known guests. Some eighteen thousand visitors a year now come to take the waters. "It's Lourdes without the religion !" said Edouard Herriot, writer and politician !

Drives through the nearby forest of Andaine and la Ferté-Macé are peaceful and relaxing. **Hound Rock** (le Roc au Chien) which juts out above the Bagnoles Gorge is so-called because, according to legend, it was there that a monster with the head of a dog used to devour young girls of marriageable age.

The phallic **Goodwill Lighthouse** (Phare de Bonvouloir) is said to have been built by a grateful lord to whom the spring had restored his youth, thereby enabling him to continue the family lineage.

To the south of Bagnoles lies **Couterne Castle,** a rather plainly-decorated construction dating back to the 16th century. It was built for Jean de Frotté, the Chancellor of Margaret of Navarre, but was refurbished and enlarged in the 18th century. During the French Revolution, a fire destroyed the precious archives of the Protestant family, and it is said that the ghost of the rebel General, Louis de Frotté, still haunts the castle. The old fortifications now form the basis of terraced gardens.

The fortress-castle of **Lassay** built in the reign of Charles VII, is the scene of a son et lumière in the summer months. Lavoisier, the chemist, stayed in the castle in the 18th century and built an oven there so that he could carry out various experiments.

BALLEROY (Calvados)
10 miles S.W. of Bayeux.

Balleroy **Castle** (1626-1636) situated on the border between the Bessin and Bocage regions, was one of the first architectural assignments ever carried out by François Mansart. It was built for Jean de Choisy, later Chancellor to Gaston d'Orléans, but was sold by his nephew, the transvestite Abbot de Choisy, in order to pay his debts.

It is an austere, majestic building at the end of the one and only village street. The plain exterior, in the Louis XIII style, gives no hint of the richly-decorated interior with the gallery of portraits by Mignard and its large library.

In the centre of the balustrade on the terrace flanking the main lodges is a subtly unusual staircase formed by two half-circles. The outbuildings are placed symetrically to either side of flowerbeds laid out by Le Nôtre. One of the buildings now houses a Hot Air Balloon **Museum.**

The parish **church,** formerly the castle chapel, is also attributed to Mansart.

BARNEVILLE-CARTERET (Manche)
37 miles N. of Coutances.

The busiest seaside resort in the Cherbourg Peninsula is actually three adjoining towns. Nestling above the natural harbour of Carteret, formed by the estuary of the R. Gerfleur and protected from the nor'westerlies by **Cape Carteret,** is the borough of **Carteret,** a sheltered fishing port and yachting marina. It is also the point of departure for trips to the Channel Islands. A narrow path worn down by customs officers of old, runs round the picturesque cliffs from Cape Carteret to the ruins of the Vieille Eglise. There is a splendid view from the top of the lighthouse, while from the Biard Rock (roche Biard), the visitor can look along the coast to Flamanville in the north and Granville in the south, or out to sea as far as Jersey.

Barneville-Carteret, which is set back from the estuary, has a Norman church with a battlemented tower dating from the 15th century. The finely-worked ornamentation on the arches and capitals along the nave consists of animal and plant motifs drawn from oriental imagery.

Situated at the southern end of the natural harbour which becomes a mudflat at low tide, **Barneville-Plage** has a long stretch of sandy beach to offer water-sports enthusiasts. The beach extends as far as **Portbail,** a quiet little harbour at the mouth of the R. Olonde. Like Barneville, it has a church with a fortified tower.

The castle-fortress in **Bricquebec,** which is very well preserved, belonged to the grand-nephew of the first Duke of Normandy and was given the finishing touches in the 13th and 14th centuries. A polygonal 14th century keep stands on a feudal motte*, surrounded by an outer wall. In the vaulted crypt of the south wing, there is a permanent exhibition of bronze sculptures by Le Véel (19th century). The clock-tower houses a regional museum which, among other items of interest, tells the story of how the apple was first introduced into Normandy.

In the centre of Cherbourg Peninsula lies **Saint-Sauveur-le-Vicomte,** a ''small country town as pretty as any Scottish village'' according to J. Barbey d'Aurevilly, the writer, who was born here. Although the town was badly damaged by air raids in 1944, parts of the old feudal **castle,** which played on important rôle in the One Hundred Years' War, are still standing. The

Gaillon : *castle gateway.*

◀ **Tessé-la-Madeleine** : *the neo-Renaissance castle of Roche-Bagnoles built in the 19th century.*

Benedictine **Abbey** was restored in the 19th century, thanks to Sister Marie-Madeleine Postel who founded the order of the Sisters of Mercy. Souvenirs and memorabilia of the writer, Barbey d'Aurevilly, are on show in the **museum** which bears his name.

BAYEUX (Calvados)
17 miles N.W. of Caen.

Bayeux is the capital of the Bessin region, rich pastureland where agriculture is of prime importance. Although not far from the Normandy Beaches, Bayeux was spared during the fierce fighting of 1944 and was the first large town to fall into Allied hands. (A waxworks museum retells the story of the Normandy Campaign.)

Originally settled by the Baiocasses, and known to be a bishopric as early as the 4th century, the town was colonised by the Normans almost at the start of their invasion (and as late as the 12th century, the poet Robert Wace in his "Roman de Rou ou Geste des Normands" is still singing about the superiority of the Normans over the French). In 905, the Norman chief, Rollo, married the governor's daughter, Pope. She gave birth to the future Duke William Long-Sword, an ancestor of William the Bastard who was later to conquer England. The event inspired a masterpiece of which the town is justly proud : the famous tapestry ascribed to Queen Matilda.

The 19th century archeologist, Arcisse de Caumont, whose work was considered as authoritative in its day, was born in Bayeux.

The most imposing of the town's historic buildings is undoubtedly Notre-Dame Cathedral. A large Romanesque church built by Bishop Odo de Couteville to replace one that had previously been burnt down, was dedicated in 1077 in the presence of the Duke, William the Conqueror. Fire again caused serious damage in 1105 ; the crypt survived, as did the towers which were skilfully incorporated into the Gothic building.

The cathedral as we see it today is a fine example of Norman Gothic architecture. The slender twin spires of the façade flank the highly-ornate 15th century Patriarch's Tower, which was restored in the 19th century and reroofed with a copper 'cap'. Buttresses support the Gothic section of the building above the Romanesque nave, and a row of arches surrounds the chevet. The richly-decorated south portal of the transept has a tympanum telling the story of Thomas à Becket.

In the **nave,** the Gothic clerestory provides a pleasing balance to the 12th century Romanesque bays, with their highly-ornate stonework showing a wide variety of friezes and stylised geometric motifs drawn from oriental art ; the corner-stones* between each bay are decorated with strange animals or people. The typically-Gothic **chancel** is flooded with light, and its capitals are a fine example of mediaevel sculpture. Beneath the chancel lies the 11th century **crypt.**

The 13th century **treasure-house** is a separate two-storey building. The **chapter-house,** which is decorated with frescoes, was paved with glazed bricks in the 15th century.

In the Deanery (Hôtel du Doyen), once the bishop's palace and now the library, the visitor can see the "Tale of the Conquest" known as **Queen Matilda's tapestry** a unique piece of work from both the historical and pictorial point of view. The whole tapestry (231ft. long and 20ins. wide) is on show in a special room. It is a sort of comic strip, retelling in detail the various stages of the Norman Conquest. According to legend, Queen Matilda herself made the tapestry, but it is more likely that the embroidery, using coloured worsted on linen (wrongly called a tapestry), was ordered from an Anglo-Saxon workshop by William's half-brother, Odo, Bishop of Bayeux, and Count of Kent. The embroidered panel was first hung around the nave of the cathedral at the Dedication Ceremony in 1077.

To the faithful, the tapestry was not only a report of the campaign, but also a means of portraying a moral and spiritual lesson. Harold Godwinson had broken his word. He had sworn on sacred relics to recognise William as King of England on the death of Edward the Confessor (see the Introduction) ; he was therefore justly punished for his bad faith by the hand of God. Fifty-eight forcefully-designed pictures, subtitled in Latin and framed by two decorative borders, recount the events with an amazing attention to detail. The sequence of pictures is ingenious and their audacity is sometimes amusing, sometimes tragic. We can see the preparations and occasionally quizzical events leading up to the Channel crossing and the Battle of Hastings. Odo himself features on the embroidery, next to William.

The Bayeux Tapestry, the detailed record of a given period, is an inspired tribute to the glory and power of a conquering people, and an exceptional record of life in the 11th century.

The **Baron-Gérard Museum** contains a collection of Bayeux porcelain and local lace.

An unusual Mining Museum, the **Molay-Littry,** shows the various techniques used to work a coal seam, in a surprising and interesting fashion.

The village church in **Tour-en-Bessin** has a finely-decorated rectangular Gothic chancel.

BEC-HELLOUIN (LE) (Eure)
13 miles N.E. of Bernay.

The Abbey of Notre-Dame-du-Bec was founded in 1034 near a stream in the Forest of

Brionne by Herluin, or Hellouin, a knight and close friend of Gilbert de Brionne, who decided to give himself up to the service of God. Several years later, a learned Italian monk by the name of Lanfranc (cf. Caen), who was teaching in Avranches, was much impressed by the community's simplicity and decided to join it. His decision was to have a substantial effect on the Abbey's development ; its sphere of influence widened and it became an important centre of religious thinking.

After the Norman Conquest, Lanfranc was appointed Archbishop of Canterbury and thus became head of the English church ; he was accompanied by monks from Bec who were given the top posts in the ecclesiastical institutions. When Herluin died, he was succeeded by Anselm, a philosopher and theologian, whose abbotship marked the climax of Benedictine Normandy. Then he too was appointed to Canterbury. The prestige of the teaching of the Bec-Hellouin, its permanence and its power thus became an integral part of the Anglo-Norman kingdom and its monks played a major part in influencing ecclesastical reform and the arts.

After a period beset by wars, the Bec Abbey again became prosperous under the reformed congregation of St Maur : the architect and sculpter Guillaume de la Tremblaye, a lay member of the community, was immensely influential. The Abbey was secularised at the time of the French Revolution and was later used as a prison, barracks, and a remount depot before being given back to the Church in 1948. Since then it has maintained very close œcumenical ties with the Church of England.

The 15th century **St Nicolas Bell-tower,** which no longer has its steeple, was the only part of the minster left standing after the demolition work of the 19th century. At the top of the tower is a balustrade decorated with pinnacles*, from which there is a panoramic view of the valley. The Classical-style **monastic buildings** form a right-angle on one side of the Courtyard of France (la cour de France) in a layout that is both orderly and well-balanced. The new **abbey church** was established in the former refectory, an 18th century building with semi-circular vaulting. It houses the tomb of Herluin. One of the doors of the former **chapter-house,** built in the 12th century and embellished in the 18th, opens onto the grand staircase which leads to the **cloisters.** They were rebuilt and decorated in the 17th century by Guillaume de La Tremblaye. One of the original Gothic doors still exists, in one corner of the cloisters.

There is a veteran and vintage car **museum** near the monastery.

Brionne, an old town on the banks of the Risle not far from the Bec Abbey, boasts the ruins of an 11th century square keep overlooking the river.

BERNAY (Eure)
19 miles E. of Lisieux.

Built on the banks of the R. Charentonne, the bustling farming community of Bernay grew up around the Benedictine monastery founded by the wife of Duke Richard II, Judith of Brittany. It was generally considered to be the first Romanesque Abbey in Normandy.

It was there that the mediaeval poet Alexandre de Bernay was born. He was the father of the alexandrine. In the 12th century, he wrote a long poem on Alexander the Great in lines of 12 syllables.

The former **abbey church** is interesting despite numerous alterations. Built as an experiment, it served as a model for the region's own style of architecture. Work started on the Benedictine-style church in 1013 under the direction of William de Volpiano (cf. Fécamp) but was interrupted and was not finally completed until the 12th century.

The outside of the church has suffered a certain amount of disfigurement : in the 17th century, the nave was shortened by the Maurist monks who removed two bays in order to build a Classical façade. Later, the north crossing was demolished to make way for a street and the chevet was bricked up. The origin of the small domes over the side-aisles is still a

Brotonne Bridge : *over the R. Seine.*

◀ **Bec-Hellouin Abbey** : *Saint-Nicholas' tower.*

mystery to historians. The unusually high nave has a ceiling instead of the more common vaulted roof. A clerestory tops a double-arched triforium leading to the roof, a feature which was to be developed to the full in Gothic architecture but which is extremely rare in Romanesque buildings. The capitals, decorated with leaves and strange figures, are among the oldest in Normandy (c. 1020).

The 16th century **administration block** has been turned into a museum, while the 17th century Maurist buildings are now used as offices.

The view from the **Mount Promenade** (Promenade des Monts) extends over the town and the R. Charentonne as it winds its way through a fertile valley.

Upstream lies the village of **Broglie** (originally called 'Chambrais') which, for the past two hundred years, has been the name of the illustrious family from the Piedmont region of Italy who took over the Louis XV **castle.** The flint and hard limestone* of which it is built, give it a rather homespun appearance. It has a famous library.

Beaumesnil Castle (which appears in « Nez de Cuir » under the name 'Le Mesnil-Royal') is reflected in the lakes dotted around the park. The writer La Varende considered it to be "the pride and joy of the Ouche Region". It is a combination of Classical and exuberant Baroque architecture, built between 1633 and 1644 using stone and brick. The central part of the castle is particularly ornate. It is owned by the Furstenberg Foundation and, thanks to its permanent links with France's National Library, it houses a **Museum of Book-binding.**

BRAY (REGION OF)

This is a geological depression formed as a result of Alpine folding followed by erosion. In fact, the Bray Region is a deep 'dip' separating the limestone plateaux of the Caux Region and Picardy. The mixture of quite discernible Jurassic soil and areas of clay has created a varied landscape of rolling hills. It is a well-drained region of woodland and rich pasture ('braye' means 'mud' or 'heavy soil' in Old French) in which dairy herds graze.

The 'capital of the Norman Alps', **Gournay-en-Bray,** which lies in the valley of the R. Epte, supplies part of France with cottage and cream cheese produced in the Gervais-Danone factory of **Ferrières.** It was a Swiss cowherd on one of the local farms who, in about 1850, first thought of the formula that Charles Gervais was to put into production on a large-scale a few years later.

To the south-east of Gournay stands the church of **Saint-Germer-de-Fly,** once part of an abbey, built in the Early Pointed style of the 12th century. Beyond the chancel and its galleries is a corridor leading out of the apsidal chapel to a second church, which was built in the reign of Saint Louis. It is modeled on the Sainte-Chapelle in Paris.

On the road to Forges lies **Beauvoir-en-Lyons** which fully justifies its nickname of 'observatory', standing as it does above the river valley.

Between the sources of the rivers Epte and Andelle, in an area of woodland and man-made lakes, is the elegant spa town of **Forges-les-Eaux,** which owes its existence to Gallo-Roman smithies. The health-giving properties of its waters with their high radioactive and iron content (recommended in the treatment of anemia and certain nervous disorders) were discovered in the 16th century. The springs in the park are still called 'Royale', 'Reinette', and 'Cardinale' in memory of the visit of Louis XIII, Anne of Austria and Cardinal Richelieu.

BROTONNE (BRIDGE, FOREST, COUNTRY PARK) (Seine-Maritime)

The **Brotonne Suspension Bridge,** opened in 1977, is a daring concrete construction nearly 1,400 yds. long which spans the R. Seine. The roadway passes some 160 ft. above the river.

It links Caudebec with the **Brotonne Forest,** which lies within a meander of the river. It is mainly beech-forest, on hilly ground.

The **Brotonne Regional Country Park,** which was set up in 1974, covers 46 sq. miles of State forest on both banks of the Seine. To the west, it extends to the Vernier Marshes, to the east and south it includes the Roumare and La Lande Forests. Several tourist attractions also lie within the Park's boundaries, e.g. Jumièges and Saint-Wandrille abbeys. The main aims of the projet are to preserve nature and historic monuments, to make local people more aware of their rich cultural heritage, and to promote local events.

CABOURG-DIVES (Calvados)

15 miles N.E. of Caen.

The seaside resort of **Cabourg** on the west bank of the R. Dives was built in 1860 to a half-moon geomtrically-inspired plan : all streets lead to the casino and the Grand Hotel. Marcel Proust was a frequent visitor at the beginning of the century ; the wealthy atmosphere of the hotel, the lay-out of the streets with their shaded villas, and the games on the sands are all depicted in the elegant Balbec described in his novel "Within a budding grove" (A l'ombre des Jeunes Filles en Fleurs).

The Boulevard des Anglais runs along the fine beach to **Cabourg Point,** a sandy peninsula sheltering the yacht basin.

On the opposite bank of the river lies the small town of **Dives,** now a centre of metal-working but once an important harbour. However, the sea is a mile further away than it was at the time of a significant historical event which took place in the town during the Middle Ages. It was, in fact, from here in the autumn of 1066 that Duke William set out on his extraordinary expedition to conquer England. His fleet, which consisted of 3,000 ships and 50,000 men, beached at Pevensey where it was joined by reinforcements from Norway, and seventeen days later the Battle of Hastings resulted in victory for William.

The list of the Conqueror's companions was engraved in **Notre-Dame church** during the 19th century. The church itself, set amid the grass and trees which have replaced the cemetery, dates back to the 14th and 15th centuries. The only exception is the crossing in the transept which was originally part of a Romanesque church. The nave has a wooden ceiling.

CAEN (Calvados)

140 miles N.W. of Paris and 63 miles N. of Alençon.

Situated 140 miles from Paris at the confluence of the rivers Orne and Odon, the county town of Calvados is also the capital of Lower Normandy. Its rôle as a cultural centre and its wide sphere of influence in the spiritual field, both of which date back to the Middle Ages, have helped to further the economic expansion of the town right up to the present time.

Recent research has revealed Gallo-Roman remains on the site of the Men's Abbey but the village of Caen was not really established until 1025. Its development is mainly due to William the Conqueror, for it was his favourite place of residence. Normandy was recaptured from the English in 1204 but the town of Caen was again attacked by Kings of England in 1346 and 1417. It was not to become French again until 1450. Although outbreaks of plague followed by the Fronde Revolt weakened the town, the most difficult moments in its history are much closer in time : after the Allied Landings on 6th June 1944, it was the target of intense air attacks which destroyed three-quarters of the town. It was finally liberated on 19th July and there followed a courageous period of reconstruction, as a result of which the town's rich artistic and architectural heritage is now set off to its best advantage.

Caen is also an important centre of trade and industry. A major steel complex obtains raw material from the many local iron mines, and the docks underwent rapid expansion after the construction of the Ouistreham Canal in the 19th century.

'Caen stone', a fairly hard oolithic limestone, has always been widely used in building projets both in the town and in the surrounding area. And as far as gastronomic delights are concerned, the town is synonymous with 'tripe à la mode de Caen' (there is a tripe-making competition every year).

Many artists were born in Caen, e.g. Sohier the architect, Malherbe the poet, the painters Jean Restout, Tournières and Lépine, and the composer Auber.

Since the last war, the area around the **castle** and remparts has been cleared so that their architecture can be properly appreciated. They have regained the true character of the buildings first erected by William the Conqueror in 1060, and later enlarged and fortified by his successors. William's son, Henry I Beauclerk, added a keep to the castle but it was almost completely destroyed under the Convention ; the only part of it left standing today is the Assizes. However, one masterpiece of Romanesque civil architecture does still exist : the **Exchequer Room** (salle de l'Echiquier) (cf. Rouen), used for ceremonials when the castle was the ducal palace and now the setting for civic receptions. The outer wall houses **St George's Chapel** which has undergone much restoration work, the **Normandy Museum,** and the **Fine Arts Museum** which has a large collection of paintings from the 15th to 20th centuries. It is also possible to walk along the remparts (the walls are mainly 15th century).

William the Bastard, later to be known as The Conqueror, was excommunicated after his marriage to one of his relatives, Matilda of Flanders. Lanfranc, a learned Italian monk then living in the monastery of the Bec-Hellouin, persuaded Rome to reverse its decision. As a penance, William and Matilda founded the monasteries which were to give the town a whole new look : the Men's Abbey and the Ladies' Abbey.

Situated in the south-west of the town, **St Stephen's church** in the **Men's Abbey**

Jumièges : *inside the ruins of Notre-Dame church.*

◀ **Caen** : *the Men's Abbey.*

(l'Abbaye aux Hommes) was begun towards 1066 by Duke William under the direction of Lanfranc, who became its first abbot before acceding to the throne of Canterbury. The austerity and plainness of the tall Romanesque façade with its end-wall flanked by two slender towers (a "harmonious Norman façade" with no trace whatever of the previous Carolingian fore-part, where everything is sacrified to the exigences of architectural simplicity) were to be copied throughout Europe, as was the starkly-majestic nave. In the 13th century, the towers were topped by elegant steeples of a Gothic style common in Normandy, and the first Gothic chancel in the region was built. It is a homogeneous construction decorated with a variety of motifs. It underwent restoration in the 17th century. The chevet also dates back to the 13th and 14th centuries. After the collapse of the 400 ft. central bell-tower, the lantern-tower was rebuilt at the beginning of the 17th century.

The Benedictine **monastic buildings,** now used as the Town Hall after housing the Malherbe Grammar School, were entirely rebuilt from 1704 onwards by Guillaume de La Tremblaye. The original woodwork is still visible in the former chapter-house, parlour and refectory. The Guard Room, the only part of the Gothic building that is left, has been restored.

The **Ladies' Abbey** (l'Abbaye aux Dames), which was founded by Queen Matilda in 1062, lies to the east of the castle. Within its walls, **Holy Trinity Church** still has the vast 11th century Romanesque nave with semi-circular arches supporting a triforium* of 12th century pointed arches. The Benedictine lay-out was strictly adhered to : on either side of the apse

61

with its barrel vaulting* are the characteristic chapels of decreasing proportions that flank the chancel. An attractive 13th century chapel and 18th century restoration of both towers have in no way detracted from the overall simplicity of the style, which can also be seen in the purely Romanesque crypt. The Queen's tomb is in the chancel. The monastic buildings now house the hospital and were rebuilt in the 18th century in the Louis XIV style.

There are a large number of historic monuments in Caen, a true indication of its development over the course of the centuries. Two of them are on busy **St Peter's Square** (place Saint-Pierre) at the foot of the castle.

Saint Peter's Church (whose imposing tower was rebuilt after 1944) was begun in the 13th century in the Gothic style, and completed three centuries later by Hector Sohier. The chevet, with its remarkably opulent ornamentation, is an outstanding example of Renaissance architecture, and more of the artist's work can be seen in the vaulting of the apsidal chapels.

Another successful transplantation of the Italian-based early Renaissance style is the inner courtyard of the **Escoville Town House** (Hôtel d'Escoville), built by the same architect between 1533 and 1538 for a rich tradesman. Its harmonious proportions are highlighted by powerful Biblical and mythological statues. The building now houses the Tourist Information Office and the Caen Education Offices.

The new **university**, a symbol of the town's reconstruction, is situated in the north of Caen. The buildings, which were opened in 1957, are classically austere and simple in design.

To the west of the town, the remains of **Ardenne Abbey**, a 12th century building and the largest Premonstratensian monastery in Normandy, now belong to two farms. The remains include the gateway and the 13th century tithe barn, a Louis XIII lodge and Classical buildings, and the church with its pure Gothic nave.

Not far away, in **Norrey,** is a little Gothic church remarkable for its 13th century chancel and richly-decorated capitals.

In the Lue Valley lies the Renaissance castle of **Lasson,** attributed to Hector Sohier who undertook the intricate ornamentation of the façade.

Nestling in a damp valley outwith the village itself, the Romanesque church of **Thaon,** which was described as "a battlemented prayer in a natural setting" (J. Roman, "Toute la Normandie", 1965), has an unusual 11th century bell-tower and a delicately-ornamented exterior. It is no longer used for worship.

In **Troarn,** a town midway along the R. Dives to the east of Caen, the remains of the Benedictine Abbey of Saint Martin show that it was stil prosperous in the 13th century, some 200 years after its foundation by Roger de Montgomery in 1048. The founder's wife, Mabile, who was well-known for her cruelty, was murdered and buried in the chancel of the abbey church.

Situated at the gateway to the Norman Alps, **Thury-Harcourt** is a good centre for touring. The 17th century castle of the Dukes of Harcourt was burnt down in 1944 and later rebuilt on the remaining foundations.

From the top of Mount Pinçon (1,185 ft.), there is a view right over the surrounding woodland and countryside.

CALVADOS (COAST) AND NORMANDY LANDING BEACHES

From Caen to Carentan, the Calvados coastline (encompassing the Mother-of-Pearl Coast from the Orne Estuary to Courseulles and the Bessin Coast from there to the R. Vire) is closely linked to the still-vivid memories of the Allied Landings during the Second World War.

Supreme command for the liberation of Europe was given to General Eisenhower, while General Montgomery had command of Allied ground forces during Operation Overlord. On the German side, Field-Marshal Rommel was in charge of coastal defences from Saint-Nazaire up to, and including, Holland, and he took his job very seriously. The Normandy region was chosen as a landing site by the 'Cossac' Allied chiefs-of-staff because of the quality of its beaches, and detailed plans were drawn up as early as 1943. The German forces had not foreseen the possibility of a landing at low tide, and especially not during a storm. In fact, bad weather delayed the Landings for twenty-four hours and they finally got underway on 6th June 1944.

Backed up by the air-borne divisions dropped overnight, preceded by heavy shelling of the beaches and their defences from the air and the sea, and aided by the coordinated actions of the Resistance movement within France which had been put on alert through a BBC broadcast (a coded poem by Verlaine), six Allied divisions landed on a beachhead some 50 miles long. From East to West, the beaches were given the code names **Sword** (English) = Ouistreham-Lion-sur-Mer ; **Juno** (Canadian) = Saint-Aubin- Courseulles ; **Gold** (English) = La Rivière-Asnelles ; **Omaha** (2 American divisions) = Sainte-Honorine-Verville ; and **Utah** (American) = La Madeleine-Saint-Germain-de-Vareville (cf. Cherbourg Peninsula).

At regular intervals, 5,000 ships put men, tanks and equipment ashore. In the evening of 'D-Day', the situation was holding by a thread but the way was clear for the invasion forces waiting in England. The long and costly Battle of Normandy was to last 77 days. A large number of military cemeteries commemorate the human lives lost by armies of various nationalities. Solid concrete defences, the remains of the 'Atlantic Wall' built by the Germans, are dotted along the coastline.

The **Mother-of-Pearl Coast** (Côte de Nacre), with its string of seaside resorts famous for their beaches and health-giving climate,is particularly suitable for swimming and on-shore fishing.

The churches of **Langrune** and **Bernières** both have 13th century bell-towers.In Bernières, it is 218 ft. high.

At the mouth of the R. Seulles (which has not always followed its present course) lies **Courseulles-sur-Mer**, the "Pride of the Mother-of-Pearl Coast". Its oysters were famous as far back as the 18th century when it used to supply the Court of Versailles. Its reputation has remained untarnished ever since. The harbour, which was much used in the 19th century, has been renovated after gradually silting up and being badly damaged in the last war (Juno Beach).

Beyond Courseulles, the shoreline is less monotonous, more varied. It was in **Arromanches-les-Bains** (Gold Beach) in June 1944 that a Mulberry Harbour, Churchill's brainchild, was built in a few days using pontoons towed across the Channel. Stretching along the coast for several miles, it enabled the landing of troops and equipment (sometimes as much 9,000 tonnes a day) for ten weeks until Cherbourg and Le Havre could be liberated. The **Allied Landings Museum** (musée du Débarquement) shows the various stages of the operation in a well-documented exhibition.

Out to sea are the **Calvados Reefs** on which the "Salvador" foundered in 1588. She was part of the Spanish Armada. It is said that the reefs got their name from one of the ships wrecked on them ; they later gave it to the county itself.

Beyond Arromanches, the **Bessin Coast** becomes very rugged, with clay cliffs and valleys reminiscent of the Caux Region, or rocky scree like the **Chaos**. Inland, however, the landscape is pastoral.

Flanked by high cliffs, **Port-en-Bessin** is a fisherman's paradise and the picturesque fish market of the professionals (open three times a week) adds to the hustle and bustle created by the amateurs. Shellfish are collected on the rocky plateaux left uncovered at low tide. There is no beach.

Omaha The Bloody. The name given to the part of the rugged coastline where German and American troops were locked in bitter combat. The storm, the wind and the currents first took the American units one-and-a-half miles away from the appointed Landing site and then

prevented the construction of the second Mulberry Harbour at **Vierville** which would have taken some of the load off the one in Arromanches.

The **American cemetery** in **Saint-Laurent** preserves the memory of nearly 10,000 men, in an impressive setting.

In **Formigny,** there was yet another battle, this one fought on 18th April 1450. It gave the victorious French troops back their confidence when they beat the English Army. The aim was the same — the Liberation of Normandy. Only the participants in the battle were different.

Near the **Bec du Hoc,** a rocky headland where the US Rangers found fame on 6th June 1944 (Utah Beach), lies the fishing port of **Grandcamp-les-Bains.**

Situated at the mouth of the rivers Vire, Taute and Douve, the **Grand Vey Bank,** a wide bay which has silted up, is a favourite spot with migrating seabirds.

At one end of the bay is **Isigny-sur-Mer,** a town famous for its toffee and butter. In addition to the dairies, maritime trade is thriving as is mussel-farming. Local stock is known as 'caïeux d'Isigny'.

Not far away is the large German cemetery of **La Cambe.**

CARROUGES (Orne)
10 miles E. of la Ferté-Macé.

On the edge of the Ecouves Forest in the heart of the 900 sq. mile Normandy-Maine Regional Park, is Carrouges Castle, an immense rectangular building flanked by towers and lodges of brick and stone, and surrounded by a moat.

There is a legend attached to the name of the castle. Count Ralph was unfaithful to his wife during her pregnancy. One day, when she came upon the lovers, she stabbed her husband's mistress, only see her disappear in a fountain for she was a fairy. A few hours later, Ralph was found with his throat cut and the countess saw a bloodstain appear on his forehead. She died in childbirth and when her son reached the age of seven, a red mark appeared on his forehead too. From that time on, he was known as Carl the Red (Karle le Rouge).

Building work continued from the 14th to the 17th century around the central courtyard. The **barbican** was built by Jean Le Veneur in the 16th century. It is said that Louis XI stayed in the castle on his way to the Mont Saint-Michel. Until 1936, it belonged to the descendants of the Carrouges, the Le Veneur de Tillières family, who then presented it to the Monuments Historiques (the French equivalent of the National Trust). A portrait gallery gives a glimpse of successive generations of Le Veneurs.

Midway between Sées and Alençon, the **Ecouves State Forest** has many picturesque and hilly footpaths like the one leading to the Vignage Rocks which overlook the woodland itself and the Alençon countryside. The forest also contains game.

At 1,368 ft. the **Signal d'Ecouves** is the highest hill in north-western France, along with the Mount Les Avaloirs.

CAUDEBEC-EN-CAUX (Seine-Maritime)
22 miles N.W. of Rouen.

The former capital of the Caux Region lies on the right bank of the R. Seine at the head of the wooded Sainte-Gertrude Valley. In the 15th century, the manufacture of felt rain hats,

Lessay : *the nave of the minster in which there are early examples of ogival arches (the arches of the first two bays, the oldest in the church, rest directly on the cornice, whereas the remainder are more skilfully constructed and are supported by capitals).*

Mont Saint-Michel : *the Guests' Room.* ▶

65

known as 'Caudebecs', was a thriving industry.

Dykes and the construction of channels in the river have done away with the tidal bore. It was from Caudebec that this phenomenon could be seen at its most spectacular (a sort of barrier was created at flood tides by the confrontation of river water rushing downstream and the rising tide running upstream). A devastating wave would then engulf the river banks, causing frequent drowning accidents like the one which brought so much grief to the Hugo and Vacquerie families (cf. Villequier).

The town had to be almost totally rebuilt after the fire in 1940 which destroyed the entire town centre with the exception of a few timber-fronted houses, the 13th century **Knights Templar's House** (Maison des Templiers) which is now the Biochet-Bréchot Museum, and the church.

King Henri IV considered **Notre-Dame church** to be "the most beautiful chapel in the whole realm". It was built in the Flamboyant style between 1426 and 1539. On the façade above the intricately-carved doors is a Renaissance gallery of caryatids and an enormous rose window. Beneath the gable, inscriptions have been carved into the stone and a balustrade runs round the whole building. The traceried bell-tower is capped by a circlet of stone which underwent restoration in the 19th century.

Inside the church, a sculpted organ loft of stone dominates the nave which is suffused with light from 16th century stained glass windows. There is no transept. The Chapel of the Holy Sepulchre is decorated with an ornate canopy. In the Lady Chapel (chapelle de la Vierge), the pointed arches which support the chevet spring from a remarkable pendant weighing 7 tonnes — a daring feat of the architect Guillaume Le Teiller, who is buried here.

To the south of Caudebec, the Brotonne bridge (q.v.) is silhouetted against the skyline. It replaced the old Seine ferry.

Further upstream, where the river meets the R. Austreberthe, the small port of **Duclair** nestles among orchards. In **Saint-Denis' church,** with its Romanesque bell-tower topped by a 16th century steeple, Gallo-Romain building materials were used in the construction of the vaulted nave in which the arches are early ogival in forme. There are, for example, four marble half-columns. The 14th century statues come from Saint Peter's in Jumièges.

'Duclair duckling', the gastronomic delight for which the area is famous, was originally produced by crossing wild ducks from the marshes and estuary with their free-range domestic cousins.

CAUX (REGION OF)

This is a vast plateau stretching from the R. Brêle to the R. Seine. The 'dip' of the Bray Region forms a notch in its north-east corner. Known as the Grand Caux between Le Havre, Rouen and Dieppe, and the Lesser Caux between Dieppe and the R. Brêle, the region was once settled by the Caleti. It is a combination of deep layers of chalk and much flint. Less fertile than the Vexin Plateau because of the impermeability of the soil, its coastline is characterised by 320 ft. chliffs which are gradually being worn away by water, wind, frost and the pebbles which are dashed against them by the incoming tide. The grandiose white wall, which looks almost manmade, is in fact receding yearly by one to six feet in some places. The remains of the original coastline can be seen one-and-a-half miles out to sea. Large crevices are formed in the rock, such as those near Dieppe known as 'gobes' which were later filled in by the Germans.

Occasionally, the receding coastline cuts into the lower reaches of dried-up streams forming the clefts known as **'valleuses'**, which are often the site of harbours. When the scree eventually covers the base of the cliffs, they are described as being 'dead'.

Along the coast, the main industry is small-scale fishing ; inland, agriculture takes pride of place beside linen scutching and cattle-breeding. The farm buildings surrounded by grassy banks, known as 'clos-masures' are a welcome sight in the otherwise monotonous countryside. An unusual farming pratice carried out in this region is the tethering of cows.

From Dieppe to Etretat where marl gives the sea a milky appearance, the line of cliffs forms the **Alabaster Coast**. The rich contrast of hue and tone have attracted many painters to this area over the years. Dotted along the meandering shoreline is a string of small holiday resorts and harbours.

The fishing port of **Saint-Valéry-en-Caux,** which grew up around a monastery founded in the 7th century by St Valéry, was a busy harbour as far back as the 11th century and later it became particularly prosperous. Today, it is popular with sailing buffs. From the Aval cliff, the view extends to Le Tréport.

To the south of Etretat, the cemetery and castle of **Cuverville** call to mind the writer André Gide who was married there.

The road to Le Havre runs through the **Lizard Valley** (vallée de la Lézarde).

CERISY-LA-FORET (Manche)

To the north-east of Saint-Lô, not far from a beech forest, lies the little village of Cerisy-la-Forêt. In its midst are the ruins of an influential Benedictine abbey which was founded in the 6th century by Vigor, later Bishop of Bayeux, and rebuilt in 1030 by Duke Robert I. It was here that the monks illuminated the writings of Saint Gregory.

Although several bays were removed from the nave during the 19th century, the Romanesque **abbey church** remains an austere yet daring exemple of mediaeval architectural research into ways of allowing light to penetrate the building.

Originally, the nave and chancel had ceilings — as have several Norman churches in England. The advantages of such a system was that the load-bearing walls could be hollowed out, since they did not have to support the weight of a vaulted roof. The windows in the galleried nave, chancel and apse are on three levels ; and in the apse, where the semi-circular wall is pierced with lights, there is a clerestory passage, which was a most unusual architectural feature in its day. The chevet is a well-balanced combination of form and strength. A lantern-tower above the transept crossing added more light to the interior but it was obscured by groined vaulting when the monks modified the chancel in the 14th century. Work presently underway is intended to restore the church's original layout.

The 13th century **monastic buildings** are still in existence. The **Abbot's Chapel,** a gift from Saint Louis, is an example of pure Gothic architecture.

CHANNEL ISLANDS

Once part of the Continental land mass, these are granite islands. The two largest, Jersey and Guernsey, are respectively the most southerly and the most westerly of the group. They can be reached by plane or boat. There are regular ferry services from Saint-Malo or the west coast of the Cherbourg Peninsula.

The other islands are Alderney to the north-east, Sark, Herm, Brecqhou, and Jethou.

Jersey, the largest and most densely-populated of the Channel Islands, is separated from the French coast by a 16-mile stretch of water. The proximity of the Gulf Stream explains the island's mild climate. Because of its ever-changing landscape (creeks and high cliffs in the north, wide sandy beaches elsewhere), it has become very popular with tourists.

The island draws its wealth mainly from market gardening and cattle-breeding, although seaweed-gathering and, more especially, fishing are also lucrative activities (shellfish, including ormers, crabs, conger eels, etc.).

Rouen : *the "crowned tower" of Saint-Ouen's church.*▶

Although the island has been an English possession since 1145, it has its own constitution and its own government. In the 18th and 19th centuries, it offered asylum to French political refugees. Many of its inhabitants are of Norman decsent. The mediaeval poet, Robert Wace, was born on Jersey.

Guarded by Castle Elizabeth, its capital, **Saint Helier,** named after the island's first evangelist, has a sheltered yacht basin and is very popular with shoppers. On the east coast stands **Mont Orgueil Castle,** high above the harbour in **Gorey.**

Guernsey's landcape is the opposite of Jersey's, for it rises from north to south and, in the south-west, the cliffs are some 390 ft. high. Whereas the western and north-eastern shorelines are ragged, the north coast is absolutely flat.

The island's history was the same as Jersey's until the 17th century when Guernsey people showed their independent spirit by supporting Cromwell against the Royalists. In the 18th century, the dreaded pirates of Guernsey, famous for the fabulous bounty they captured, and local smugglers ensured the prosperity of the island. Today, however, its wealth is based on cattle and market gardening, particularly under glass.

Although Guernsey is more anglicised than Jersey, its laws are still based on Norman common law.

Victor Hugo spent some fifteen years in exile on Guernsey. His residence, **Hauteville House,** contains a collection of memorabilia.

As in the case of Jersey, vestiges of fortifications remind the visitor of the German occupation during the Second World War.

The houses in the capital, **Saint Peter Port,** are built up in tiers above the harbour. There is fishing both here and in **Saint Sampson. Castle Cornet,** which was fortified in the 13th century, underwent alterations in the 16th.

CHAUSEY (ISLES) (Manche)

Off Granville.

A fifty-five minute boat trip from Granville takes the visitor to the granite archipelago of the Isles Chausey, a paradise for shellfish gatherers. At high tide, some fifty islands and rocks jut out from the sea ; when the tide ebbs, there are as many as there are days in the year.

Only one of the islands is inhabited and open to tourists : the **Grande Ile,** one-and-a-half miles long and half-a-mile wide, covered in moorland and gorse. The only buildings in the tiny fishing village are a chapel, two hotels, a lightouse, a fort and an old castle restored by Louis Renault.

Chausey granite was quarried for many years. One outstanding example of its use as a building material is the Mont Saint-Michel.

CHERBOURG (Manche)

48 miles N.W. of Saint-Lô.

The strategic position of Cherbourg at the tip of the peninsula that bears its name prompted Vauban to turn his attention to the possibility of fortifying the town as far back as 1686. However, Cherbourg's use as a naval and berth for Transatlantic liners dates from the work carried out in the reign of Louis XVI, to forestall landings by British expeditionary forces, and the larger-scale installation work ordered by Napoleon I and finally inaugurated by Napoleon III in 1858.

In addition to the forts on **Pelée Island** and **Querqueville Point,** a huge deep sea-wall was sunk off-shore (in the presence of Louis XVI during his only trip to the provinces before his flight to Varennes), forming a vast manmade harbour. Within it, extra protection is afforded by the Homet Fort.

Cherbourg was completely cleared of mines by the Allied Forces in 1944 and thereafter played a vital rôle in supplying the troops : petrol was brought from the Isle of Wight by 'PLUTO' ('Pipe Line Under The Ocean').

Alongside its military activites (the dockyard specialises in the construction of nuclear and conventionnal submarines), Cherbourg has developed commercially and as a passenger terminal. Its quays can take the very largest ocean liners. Regular ferry crossings to England add to the hustle and bustle of the ferry and liner terminal. During the summer, yachts from many nations bob at their moorings beside the fishing smacks in the outer harbour, for Cherbourg is the second most popular yacht basin in France after Cannes.

From the 365 ft. Montagne du Roule south of the town, there is a panoramic view of the docks and the harbour basin. The **War and Liberation Museum** (Musée de la Guerre et de la Libération) is housed in the 19th century fort which was occupied by the German forces in 1944.

The **Thomas Henry Museum of Fine Arts** (Musée des Beaux-Arts) contains some thirty paintings, drawings and engravings by J.-F. Millet, who was born in the nearby hamlet of Gruchy.

The Emmanuel-Liais Gardens which were created by a 19th century naturalist, contain a variety of trees from the Tropics, for the Gulf Stream produces mild climatic conditions.

To the east of Cherbourg, the picturesque Renaissance castle of **Tourlaville** with its colourful park is reflected in the waters of its moat. Built at the end of the 16th century by Abbot Hambye and his brother, it was the scene of an incestuous love affair between Julien and Marguerite de Ravalet which ended tragically in 1603 : because of their immoral act, and despite their youth (they were aged 21 and 17), the lovers were excuted on the Place de Grève.

CHERBOURG PENINSULA

The entire Cherbourg, or Cotentin, Peninsula, formed of granite and shale, and battered by the winds, lies within the county boundaries of Manche, and its 200-mile coastline gives it a rather independent character quite unlike that of the rest of Normandy. Indeed, some of its wild rugged countryside is more reminiscent of Ireland or Scotland.

The variations in soil and geographical features are caused by its position midway between the Paris Basin and the Armorican Mountains. The Lower Cotentin, around Carentan, is a marshy grassy depression where castle-breeding is the main industry and whose wealth in bygone days came from the extraction of peat. It draws off most of the waterways as far as the alluvial plateau of Saint-Mère-Eglise (known as the **Plain**). In the north-east of the peninsula, beyond Valognes, the Saire Valley has a quite different, rather mild climate. It is an area of fruit-farms and market gardens. To the west of Cherbourg are the indented cliffs of La Hague.

The sea has always played a predominant rôle in the peninsula's history. It was occupied by the Romans in the 1st century B.C. and later overrun by Germanic tribes, then by Saxons and Vikings. From time to time, it was invaded by the English. In 1944, the Allied Forces again came by sea, this time as liberators.

From an economic point of view, the Cherbourg peninsula is important for its agriculture especially dairy farming and meat production, with some vegetable farming and cider apple orchards. While the busy harbours of Cherbourg and Granville cater for goods and passenger traffic, other ports are used by small inshore fishing fleets.

It was to the north-east of **Carentan,** which is a centre of dairy farming and horse-breeding, in the area known as **Utah Beach** (cf. Normandy Beaches), that the Americans landed on 6th June 1944 as air-borne troops were being dropped round **Sainte-Mère-Eglise,** the first town to be liberated. This is the area in which the Norman breed of cattle was first developed, but as a battle zone its terrain was somewhat less attractive. Its woodland and dense

Cerisy-la-Forêt : *the minster.*

◀ **The Norman Perche region** : *a typical landscape.*

undergrowth hindered the progress of the Allied Forces and enabled the enemy to put up resistance from sheltered positions : this was 'hedge warfare'.

In the **Saire Valley** where woodland breaks up the stretches of pasture and orchard, the mild climate has produced a pleasing combination of coastal and rural landscapes.

Opposite **Tatihou Island**, the picturesque fishing and yachting harbour of **Saint-Vaast-la-Hougue** is a centre of large-scale shellfish and oyster-farming. Twice in the past it has been the scene of important events. First of all, Edward III landed here in 1346 when, as part of his attempt to seize the crown of France, he undertook the conquest of Normandy. In the 17th century, Vauban built **La Hougue Fort** at the end of a seawall, after the disastrous sea battle of 1692 which opposed the Anglo-Dutch and French fleets. Tourville had been nominated by Louis XIV to set James II back on the throne of England, but his ships were thrown off course by storms. They foundered on the rocks and were set on fire.

From the top of **La Pernelle Hill,** there is a panoramic view over the countryside and **Réville Bay.** In fine weather, the Calvados coast is visible to the naked eye.

Beyond **Saire Point,** the granite coastline becomes rugged and wild. Legend has it that the breakers which smash against the rocks bring with them the mournful cries of a local monk condemned to wander through eternity because of a malicious lie he once told about his father's tenant farmers.

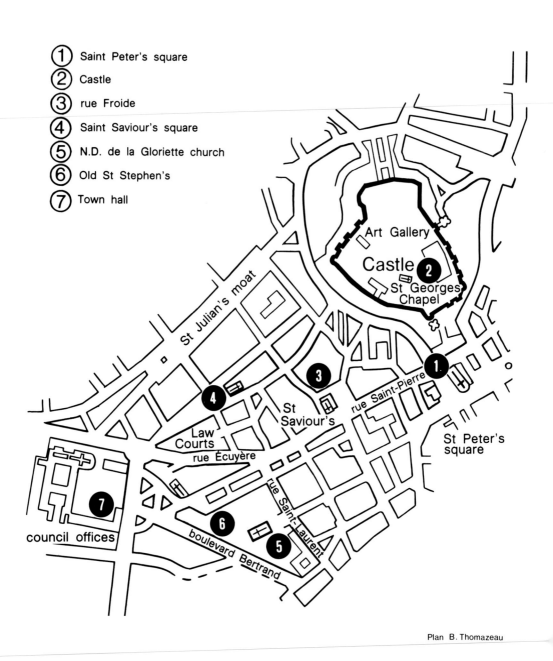

1. Saint Peter's square
2. Castle
3. rue Froide
4. Saint Saviour's square
5. N.D. de la Gloriette church
6. Old St Stephen's
7. Town hall

Caen : *town plan.*

Rouen : *town plan.*

Plan B. Thomazeau

Creully : *the keep of the fortress-castle with its Renaissance round tower.*

◀ Lisieux : *Saint-Teresa's basilica, a much-frequented place of pilgrimage and one of the largest churches built in the 20th century.*

Barfleur, a traditional fishing port and seaside resort, has a yacht basin and up-to-date rescue equipment. It was off the coast here, where the wind is blustery and the currents particularly strong, that the "Blanche Nef" foundered in 1120 with the friends and family of King Henry I of England on board. The reefs are clearly visible from the **Barfleur Point** lighthouse. In Barfleur itself, there is a small pottery which still uses wood for firing its ceramics.

79

The historian Alexis de Tocqueville wrote his books in **Tocqueville Castle,** a traditional Saire Valley shale building which has undergone alterations more than once in its life.

In **Saint-Pierre-Eglise,** an 18th century castle replaced the one where the Abbot de Saint-Pierre, author of the original project for everlasting peace, was born in 1658.

The modern **Cape Lévy** lighthouse overlooks the Cherbourg basin and the Cap de La Hague.

On the high rocky plateau of **La Hague,** the landscape is wild, grandiose, broken, and desolate, a mixture of ragged cliffs hollowed out by caves, and deserted moorland. Barbey d'Aurevilley described it as "a much beloved bitch of an area", in sharp contrast to the "smiling" Saire Valley portrayed by René Bazin. The difference is increasingly marked by small creeks and a few fertile valleys. There are very few harbours along the barren shoreline.

The Channel Islands were once part of the Continental land mass, though isolated by falls of rock. This barrier now causes violent eddies out in the deep and they, in turn, produce the terrible current known as the **'Blanchard Race'** (Raz Blanchard).

A huge dyke, the Hague-Dick, used to cut the peninsula in two and some parts of it are still visible. It was built as protection against invasion by land, not by sea, and is thought to be the work of the Celts. The Vikings are said to have made use of it at a later date.

Near the village of **Gréville** within whose jurisdiction lies Gruchy where the painter of "The Angelus", J.-F. Millet, was born, **Castel-Vendon Rock** juts out into the sea.

Not far from the **Cap de La Hague,** the lifeboat station in **Goury** keeps a weather eye on any shipping passing through the Blanchard Race.

The cliff which runs along **Ecalgrain Bay** with its view over Alderney, Sark and Guernsey, leads to the craggy rocks of the **Nez de Jobourg,** an imposing headland towering some 400 ft. above the reefs.

Near the deserted cove at **Vauville** are the remains of a Neolithic gallery, way off the beaten track in the middle of the moors. It is known as the 'Pierres Pouquelées'.

Down as far as Carteret, the landscape of the west coast of the Cherbourg Peninsula is varied : high cliffs and caves separated by sand dunes, themselves interspaced by depressions. The only harbour is **Diélette.**

From the rugged cliffs of **Cape Flamanville,** the highest spot in the area, there is a panoramic view of the Channel Islands. Nearby stands the granite **castle of Flamanville,** a 17th century building which was constructed on the ruins of a former manor-house. In 1778, a close friend of J.-J. Rousseau had a lodge built in the grounds so that the writer could spend his old age here ; in fact, he never came.

CONCHES-EN-OUCHE (Eure)

11 miles S.W. of Evreux.

The village overlooks a meander of the R. Rouloir in a wooded part of the Ouche Region. Conches is the Old French word for a shell, and it was this same word which provided the name for the village of Conques in Aquitaine which is famous for its minster, St. Faith's. It was in 1034 on his way home from Spain that Roger de Tosny made a pilgrimage to the village, bringing with him the relics of the saint to whom he dedicated the church.

Not far from the ruins of a 12th-century cylindrical keep stands the Flamboyant and Renaissance-style **St. Faith's Church** (église Sainte-Foy), built to replace the original place of worship in the 15th and 16th centuries. One of the towers on the façade, with its finely-sculpted bell-tower, was rebuilt in the 19th century ; the other tower was never completed.

A homogeneous set of stained glass windows dating from the 16th century decorate the side aisles in the nave and chancel. The ones depicting the lives of Christ and St. Faith in the chancel are attributed to an artist from Beauvais, Romain Buron, who drew his inspiration from the work of the German masters, including Dürer.

COUTANCES (Manche)
17 miles W. of Saint-Lô.

Situated on a hilltop in a wooded area in the south of the Cherbourg, or Cotentin, Peninsula, Coutances was its main religious centre as far back as Roman times. Indeed, Coutances and Cotentin are both derived from the name of the emperor, Constans I.

The cathedral was pillaged several times over the centuries and suffered severe damage in 1944. It was rebuilt by L. Arretche, who was instrumental in the reconstruction of Saint-Malo.

The **Cathedral of Our Lady** (Notre-Dame) was built in the 13th century by bishops Hugues de Morville and Jean d'Essey on the site of a Romanesque church whose foundation-stone had been laid in 1030 by Geoffroy de Montbraye. This earlier building was completed thanks to the generosity of the sons of Tancrède de Hauteville, founders of the Kingdom of Sicily. Now, the elegant graceful and harmonious lines of the cathedral make it one of the finest examples of Gothic architecture in the whole of Normandy. Vauban called it "a sublime piece of folly".

However, the Romanesque building has not completely disappeared. Although the twin towers, linked by a balustrade known as the "Rose Gallery", are decorated in the Gothic style and have been heightened for extra effect, their foundations date from an earlier period and are still visible inside the church. The towers are flanked by elongated pinnacles with tapering lights, called "fillettes", which produce an overall impression of lightness. A tall lantern-tower, the "Plomb", crowns the chevet. It is an audacious piece of work but its decoration is both subtle and refined.

The sense of verticality and daring is further present in the nave where numerous ribs spring from clusters of colonettes, thereby increasing the general aspect of the building. Above the blind storey is a sculpted balustrade. At the crossing, the vault of the lantern-tower is 125 ft. high, suffusing the High Altar with light. The simple chancel has two ambulatories ; the vaulting in the second of these is skilfully connected to that of the adjoining chapels.

The Renaissance lantern-tower of **Saint Peter's Church** (église Saint-Pierre), which is reminiscent of the papal triple crown, serves as a reminder of the help given to the building project by Pope Alexandre VI.

From the terraced footpaths of the **Public Park,** once the gardens of the Morinière House, the visitor can see the remains of a mediaeval aqueduct.

CREULLY-SAINT-GABRIEL-BRECY (Calvados)
6 miles N.W. of Caen.

Between the Bessin Region and the Caen area, in a transitional belt dotted with picturesque old windmills, the fortress-castle of **Creully** stands above the Seulles river valley. In addition to its 12th and 13 th centuries outer fortifications, there are a number of buildings including a 16th century round tower adjoining the keep, and Louis XIII stables.

It should not be confused with the nearby **Creullet** Castle, a more recent building used by Field Marshal Montgomery as his headquarters in June 1944.

In the hamlet of **Brécy,** there is a small castle with a magnificent gateway, set in terraced gardens. It is reminiscent of the great Mansart's style. Not far away are the ruins of **Saint-Gabriel-Brécy Priory.**

It was a rather distant daughter-house of the Abbey of Fécamp, founded in the 11th century by one of its monks, Vital, the son of the Lord of Creully. The Priory was, in fact, an

Yport (nr. Fécamp) : *chalk cliffs.*

abbey in its own right, given the size of its monastic buildings (now a horticultural centre), its gate-house and its **church.**

Only the Romanesque chancel of the church remains intact. Its refined ornamentation is very unusual ; sculptures and geometrical motifs cover every inch of available space, highlighting the architectural design.

A two-storey tower, the priory's seat of justice, strengthened and provided protection for the group of buildings around it. The vaulted room that was once the refectory has also been preserved.

DEAUVILLE-TROUVILLE (Calvados)
18 miles N. of Lisieux.

On the banks of the R. Touques lie the famous seaside resorts of Deauville and Trouville, displaying the elegance and luxury which is so attractive to the Parisian smart set and, indeed, to visitors from all over the world. Although the towns are popular with the Beautiful People, they also cater for sportsmen and women with up-to-date facilities and a large number of competitions.

The small port of **Trouville** was already a favourite haunt of painters and writers in the mid-19th century (visitors included Isabey, Dumas, and Flaubert who met the love of his life, Mme Schlesinger, here). Under the Second Empire, it became a meeting-place for the intellec-

Lonlay-l'Abbaye : *the church porch.*

tual and artistic élite. Boudin has immortalised the wide beach dotted with figures silhouetted against contrasting backgrounds, while in his series "Remembrance of Things Past" (A la Recherche du Temps Perdu) Proust describes the Hotel des Roches which figures so often in the work of successive generations of artists who have been attracted to the resort.

Outwith the tourist season, the little town is busy in other ways. The fishing industry is particularly active, providing fresh fish and seafood.

Deauville, nicknamed the '21st. arrondissement of Paris', is basically a summer resort, although the peak season is getting progressively longer. The atmosphere is both varied and colourful. There is the vast sandy beach ; the casino ; the race course where the 'Grand Prix Hippique' is run at the end of August ; the international sales of yearlings (18-month-old colts) ; the famous 'boards', the meeting-place of the regular visitors and a sight not to be missed by the inquisitive newcomer.

A row of Napoleon III-style villas remind the visitor that the resort was made famous by the Emperor's half-brother, the Duke of Morny. Large opulent houses testify to the town's development at the beginning of this century.

At the mouth of the R. Touques, the new **Port-Deauville** marina has moorings for more than one thousand yachts.

A climb to the top of **Mount Canisy,** Deauville's 'observation platform', enables the visitor to get a view of the whole Floral Coast. Its name is aptly evocative of the area's natural beauty, for beyond the sloping wooded region of Villers, the hinterland is covered in orchards.

To the north, the **Normandy Cliffs** (Corniche Normande) run down to Honfleur amid luxurious vegetation. The geological structure of the cliff near **Villerville** has recently become apparent : after the hard frosts of January 1982, a landslip suddenly opened up a wide fault about half-a-mile long.

DIEPPE (Seine-Maritime)

35 miles N.E. of Rouen.

Dieppe is not only the nearest seaside resort to Paris (an honour it shares with Le Tréport), it is also the oldest resort in France. It became fashionable at the time of the Restoration thanks to the Duchess of Berry, and was popular with Parisian trend-setters in the fields of art and letters.

Far back in its history, the strategic and commercial value of its harbour, situated at the foot of chalk cliffs on the Arques Estuary, was recognised by privateers, colonisers, explorers, fishermen and ship-owners alike. One of the latter, Jean Ango, was maritime adviser to François I who appointed him governor of the town. Rebuilt by Louis XIV after being bombarded by the Anglo-Dutch fleet in 1694, the town again suffered severe damage during the Allied Commando Raid in 1942.

In addition to its busy fishing port and commercial harbour specialising in the fruit and vegetable trade, Dieppe is also a passenger terminal. The numerous ferry links with England have ensured that the outer harbour area, surrounded on all sides by tall buildings, is a scene of intense activity.

Ivory-carving has remained a speciality of Dieppe and the museum contains some traditional examples of this meticulous craft.

St James' Church (église Saint-Jacques) was burnt down in 1195, almost as soon as building work had started, and thereafter the reconstruction lasted for several centuries. Only the transept is Romanesque ; the rest is Gothic. The impressive chevet contains 16th century Renaissance chapels. The side chapels gifted by ship-owners or members of the bourgeoisie are closed off by Flamboyant railings. The radiating chapels display a spectacular blend of two architectural styles. Ango is buried in one of them, and a frieze taken from his palatial residence in Dieppe is a reminder of his travels to far-off lands.

Overlooking the town and the beach is the **castle**, a granite and shale fortress which has been considerably altered over the course of its history. Only one tower remains of Richard I's original building. Enlarged in the 16th and 17th centuries, refurbished by Vauban, it was the governor's house before being used as a prison. Nowadays, it houses the municipal museum.

In the heart of a forest of tall trees near Dieppe stands an elegant stone and brick **castle** once beloging to Louis XVI's Chancellor, Hue de **Miromesnil.** It was here that the author Guy de Maupassant was born in 1850 and that he spent his early childhood.

Four miles inland from the coast, the castle and, indeed, the name of **Arques-la-Bataille** are reminders of the famous victory, in 1589, of Henri IV, then King of France, over the Duke of Mayenne who coveted the throne. Although the King's troops were unable to fire on the enemy because of thick fog, the castle's cannon forced the soldiers of the League to retreat. A monument in **Arques Forest** commemorates the event.

The **stronghold** itself, of which only a 12th century keep and some towers are still standing, was constructed in the 11th century and rebuilt in 1123 by Henry I of England. It was later fortified and enlarged on several occasions. It stands on a narrow rocky promontory surrounded by a moat. From the path above the moat, there is a view across the valley.

Notre-Dame Church, built in the 16th century in the Flamboyant Gothic style, has a Renaissance rood-screen.

DOMFRONT (Orne)
25 miles S.E. of Vire.

The mediaeval town of **Domfront** which derives its name from the hermit, Saint Front, is built on a strategic site overlooking the Varenne Valley. It is the capital of the Passais region, where orchards abound and where 'poiré', a strong pear-based beverage, is as popular as cider.

The fortress built by William I of Bellême and restored by Henry I Beauclerk now lies in ruins. From the garden of the keep, there is a view over the surrounding countryside.

At the foot of the town, the daughter-church of Lonlay, **Our-Lady-on-the-Water** (Notre-Dame-sur-l'eau) is an outstanding example of the simplicity and regularity of Romanesque architecture, despite the fact that part of the nave was removed in the 19th century to make way for road-widening. It is built in the shape of a Latin cross and has a solid austerely-decorated central tower. Narrow slit-windows allow the light to filter into the granite building.

Nearby, the church of the Benedictine abbey of **Lonlay,** founded in 1017 by William de Bellême, is still standing and has recently undergone restoration. Visitors pass through a 15th century porch which leads directly into the Romanesque transept with its decorated capitals. The unusually long Gothic chancel is now used as a nave.

EAWY (FOREST)

The Eawy State Forest covers some 25 sq. miles in the heart of the Bray Region. It is composed mainly of beech trees and consists, in fact, of three forests covering gently-sloping terrain : Nappes Forest, Le Croc Forest and Eawy Forest itself, which stretches the length of the Varenne river valley.

The **Limousin Ridge** (ligne des Limousins) is the backbone of the forest. From here, a number of roads and footpaths wend their way through narrow sinuous valleys.

ECOUIS (Eure)
Approx. 25 miles N.E. of Evreux.

Situated in the Norman Vexin region, Ecouis has a church containing a representative collection of 14th century sculptures thanks to Enguerrand de Marigny, one of Phillip the Fair's ministers, who was a patron of local craftsmen.

The Gothic-style **Notre Dame collegiate church,** which was founded by this lover of the arts, has a wide nave with no side aisles ; the vaulting was replaced in the 18th century.

The church was originally decorated with 52 statues, all donated by Marigny, but some of them were destroyed or stolen during the French Revolution. There is a freedom of corporal expression and a harmony of line in the work, proof of skilfully-mastered techniques. The results of this craftsmanship are moving as, for example, in the statues of Saint Veronica or Saint Agnes (also said to be Mary Magdalene or Saint Mary of Egypt) covered by her long wavy tresses. The marble tomb of Jean de Marigny, archbishop of Rouen and Enguerrand's brother, is a surprisingly realistic likeness. Other statues, in wood or stone, dating from the end of the 14th to the 17th century, complete the collection. The choir stalls are 14th century ; the woodwork in the transept is 18th century.

G. Pillemont in his "La France Inconnue" (pub. 1959) mentions an enigmatic inscription taken from one of the flagstones. It reads, "Here lie the child, the father, the sister, the brother, the wife and the husband but only two bodies repose here". A man had unwittingly married the daughter he had had eighteen years previously by his own mother (the girl was therefore his sister). When the couple discovered their family ties, they both died of broken hearts.

Fontaine-Henry : *the castle.*

Pont-L'Evêque : *the tower of Saint-Michael's church.* ▶

EPTE (VALLEY OF)

The Epte, which is a tributary of the R. Seine, rises near Forges-les-Eaux. Its course marks the boundary of the Vexin region and once formed the frontier of the Duchy of Normandy, which came into legal existence in 911 with the Treaty of **Saint-Clair-sur-Epte** signed by Rollo the Viking and Charles the Simple, King of France. The river therefore became of prime importance in battles between French monarchs and Dukes of Normandy who had become Kings of England. Fortresses ensured the defence of the right bank for the English sovereigns.

At the confluence of the pleasant river valleys of the Epte, Troësne and Révillon, stands **Gisors** which was reputed to be impregnable. The site was chosen at the end of the 11th century by Duke William the Redhaired because of its strategic position at the very heart of this region of woodland and forest. Now the capital of the Vexin, it has been rebuilt after suffering a great deal of damage in the last war.

The **fortress** is a remarkable example of Norman military architecture, combining the search for knightly prestige with the necessities of defence. Building work started in 1097 under Robert de Bellême, but the stronghold underwent alteration several times particularly under Henry II Plantagenet and Philippe Auguste who had recaptured it in 1193. It is said that the Knights Templars buried their treasure somewhere beneath the castle during their stay there from 1158-1161. Since that time, there have been many excavations carried out in great secrecy.

Within the vast semi-circular outer walls dating from the 12th and 13th centuries, flanked by towers, and in the midst of what are now gardens, stands a feudal motte*. On top of the motte is an 11th and 12th century polygonal **keep** with scant foundations but powerful piers to reinforce the construction. A solid wall runs round the fortress and near this wall are the ruins of the expiatory **chapel** dedicated to Thomas à Becket by Henry II.

The **Prisonner's Tower** (tour du prisonnier), the mightiest of all those in the outer walls, was built by Philippe Auguste as a second keep. It is cylindrical, 90 ft. high, and has three storeys of ogival arches. Beneath the upper room, which has a fireplace with an oven, was a cellar. The dungeon is on the lower storey and is lit by slit-sindows. Its walls are covered with strange graffiti and bas-reliefs drawn by prisoners.

Saint Gervais and Saint Protais Church is a combination of all the religion architectural styles introduced between the 13th and 16th centuries. The Gothic chancel and flat chevet were rebuilt along with the central tower by Blanche de Castille after a fire in 1240, and were completed in the 16th century by chapels decorated in the Renaissance style. The portals of the transept are Flamboyant, as is the nave, but the main façade, which was decorated by three members of the Grappin family of artists, is pure Renaissance. The delicately-sculpted porch is flanked by two towers, one of which has never been completed. The interior is a harmonious example of elaborate Flamboyant and Renaissance decoration, statuary and stained glass.

After Claude Monet had sailed up the river in his barge-studio painting scenes of life on the river banks, the Epte Valley became popular with a number of artists who felt drawn to Impressionism.

It was on his estate, **Giverny,** near the confluence of the Epte and the Seine, where he lived from 1883 until his death in 1926, that Monet painted the ''Water Lilies'' which now hang in the Orangerie Art Gallery in Paris. He also completed a large number of canvasses depicting the colourful garden ; some of these paintings now belong to the Marmottan Museum. The artist's house and garden, bequeathed to the Institute by this nephew, have been fully restored and, since 1980, visitors have been able to stroll round the lily pond which draws its water from the R. Epte, or cross the Japanese bridge laden with wisteria.

ETRETAT (Seine-Maritime)
17 miles N. of Le Havre.

In Etretat, a very popular summer resort with the British, the white cliffs of the Caux Region are quite spectacular. The sea has gradually sculpted the limestone and silex into architectural shapes. The beach is made of pebbles, pieces of silex which have been worn away, broken up, polished and rolled over and over by the movement of the waves. 19th century artists and writers made the little fishing port fashionable. It is a combination of contrasting colours built on a site left after cliff subsidence.

On the top of the **Upstream Cliff** (Falaise d'Amont), the modern chapel of **Our Lady of Caring** (Notre-Dame de la Garde), protector of seamen, stands next to the **Nungesser and Coli Museum.** In 1927, the two airmen tried to cross the Atlantic non-stop in their plane, the ''White Bird''. Their attempt was unsuccessful. From the observation platform, there is a view right along the coast.

A footpath leads to the South Cliff and the **Downstream Gateway** (Porte d'Aval), a huge arcade worn away in the rock. The impressive panorma includes the **Etretat Needle** (Aiguille d'Etretat), a sharp-pointed rock jutting out of the sea. It is said that there is a cave in the rock in which M. Leblanc's hero, Arsène Lupin, used to hide. The **Manneporte,** a monumental arch 280 ft. high, lies further to the left. The view extends as far as Cape Antifer.

EURE (VALLEY OF)
The R. Eure rises in the Perche Region and meanders through the Paris Basin before

finally flowing through Normandy again. It runs along the boundary then wends its way through a fertile valley dotted with villages until it joins the R. Seine at Pont-de-l'Arche.

Not far from Anet (Diane de Poitiers' castle, which is in the Ile-de-France on the other side of the river), the town of **Ivry-la-Bataille**, which was originally a fortress on the left bank of the Eure, owes its name to the famous victory of King Henri IV over the Duke of Mayenne and his Leaguers on 14th March 1590, just a few months after his victory at Arques-la-Bataille. An obelisk erected in the reign of Napoleon commemorates the event. Of the **Abbey** founded in 1071, all that remains is a large 12th century Romanesque door, showing that the art of the sculptor was no longer purely Norman ; he was obviously influenced by the work carried out at Chartres, i.e. in France.

Downstream lies **Pacy-sur-Eure** with its fine Gothic church dating back to the 13th century, **Saint Aubin's**. The altar made of glass pulp and the stained glass windows in the chancel are the work of a contemporary artist, F. Décorchemont.

The hamlet of **Cocherel** was greatly loved by Aristide Briand, who often came to stay there until his death on 1932. He is buried in the village cemetery. In the reign of Charles V, another politician had already made the village famous : it was in Cocherel that, on 16th May 1364, as part of his campaign to recapture Normandy, the constable Du Guesclin was victorious over the troops of England and Navarre.

The castle of **La Croix-Saint-Leufroy** is composed of the 17th century monastic buildings of the former **Croix-Saint-Ouen Abbey** founded in 788. After a grandiose vision which came to him while on his travels, Ouen the Bishop of Rouen planted a cross in the ground on this spot.

EVREUX (Eure)
34 miles S. of Rouen.

The county town of Eure is a rapidly-expanding bustling urban community in the valley of the R. Iton, situated near forests in the heart of a rich agricultural area. The traditional cottage craft which played such an important rôle in the town's development in the 19th century (the manufacture of ticking), has been replaced by a variety of new, thriving industries.

And yet history has by no means been kind to the town : it has suffered invasion by the Barbarians, fires, war damage, and air raids in 1944. A particularly bloody episode occurred in 1194, during the reign of John Lackland. Full of remorse for having sold the city to the king of France during Richard the Lionheart's absence, he treacherously had the entire garrison and its leaders butchered. He then fled before Philippe Auguste, who burnt the town to the ground as a measure of reprisal.

To the south of the 3rd century Gallo-Roman walls, stands **Notre-Dame Cathedral** displaying all the styles developed from the 12th to the 17th centuries in its remarkable set of stained glass windows. They are a true reflexion of the town's past ; there were prosperous times, there were troubled times.

Construction work on the cathedral lasted for many years, ending with the building of the South Tower in the 17th century. The Renaissance West Front, flanked by two towers, is quite different to the North portal built by Jean Cossart (early 16th century), which is an outstanding example of Flamboyant Gothic ornamentation.

The narrow Romanesque **nave** is linked by an oblique span to the wider Gothic **chancel** which is closed off by an 18th century grille and lit by tall 14th and 15th century windows. The carved stalls were a gift to the church in 1388 from Charles the Bad. The ambulatory chapels have highly-ornate Renaissance wooden rails. The Lady Chapel, a gift from Louis XI, contains a set of 15th century stained glass windows and several statues.

Fontaine-Guérard : *remains of the abbey.* ▶

Saint Taurin's Church, a former Benedictine minster on the site of the grave of the saint who was the first bishop of Evreux, underwent alterations that transformed it into a Gothic building. It nevertheless preserved its Romanesque crypt and crossings. In addition to the stained glass windows which retell the life of the saint, his relics are preserved in a famous reliquary which was gifted by Saint Louis. It is a masterpiece in gilded silver and enamel created in the 13th century, representing the Sainte Chapelle in miniature.

Adjacent to the cathedral is the former palace of Bishop Raoul du Fou, now the **museum.** It houses an exhibition of archeological finds, mainly from Old Evreux, the site of the Gallic settlement of the Eburovices.

EVRON (Mayenne)
37 miles S.W. of Alençon.

This small industrial town, which also has an important cattle market, once possessed a Benedictine Abbey. The 18th century buildings and **Notre-Dame Church** are still in existence.

A mighty 11th century tower dominates the church. Inside, the Romanesque nave combines with Gothic surroundings such as the highly-ornate chancel. In the Chapel of **Our Lady of the Thorn** (Notre-Dame-de-l'Epine), a statue of the Virgin holding the miraculous thorn brought back from Bethlehem by a pilgrim, stands next to the basilica's **treasure** as a reminder of the church's origin.

From the top of the **Montaigu Rise** (butte de Montaigu), there is a view that extends over the Coëvron Hills and the nearby forests.

FALAISE (Calvados)
21 miles S.E. of Caen.

The small town of Falaise overlooking the Ante Valley, suffered badly during the battle between the Allied armies and the German forces which lasted from June to August 1944.

However, the town's name had been written on the pages of History long before that date. Legend has it that it was from a window in the castle that Duke Robert the Magnificent, also known as Robert the Devil, caught sight of Arlette, the young washerwoman, as she made her way to the fountain (which still exists). Their relationship produced a famous son, William, later to be nicknamed the Conqueror. He was a patron and protector of his native town ; it was he who instigated the fairs in **Guilbray,** one of the suburbs.

The fortress on the sandstone promontory facing **Mount Myrrha** on the opposite bank of the R. Ante, is protected by a 13th century wall which originally had fourteen towers.

Isolated by a deep moat, the large rectangular **keep** (grand donjon) is the work of William's son, Henry I Beauclerk ; it was built in the 12th century. With its slender buttresses, it remains an impressive sight despite the loss of the roof and flooring. On the upper storey, the bay windows once lit his Lordship's apartments. The **small keep** (petit donjon) is adjacent to it and, although similar in style, is of a later period. The **Talbot Tower** (early 13th century), which is linked to the main keep by a curtain wall, was put up in the reign of Philippe Auguste. It has five storeys and its walls are 13ft thick.

Holy Trinity Church (église de la Trinité), at present undergoing restoration, is a combination of the Gothic, Flamboyant and Renaissance styles, the latter being visible in the flying buttresses and piers of the chevet, and a porch with panelled vaulting*.

Out in the country near Falaise lies the Classical castle of **Versainville,** now the 'Talbot Children's Centre', but once the property of the Intendant Fouquet.

FECAMP (Seine-Maritime)
25 miles N.E. of Le Havre.

Situated in a narrow valley between the high cliffs of the Alabaster Coast, Fécamp owes its expansion to Holy Trinity Monastery, Benedictine liqueur, and its busy harbour.

In the 7th century, Duke Waninge founded a convent on the site of the sanctuary containing the relics of the Precious Blood gathered by Joseph of Arimathea. The relics are said to have been hidden in the trunk of a fig tree and set adrift. They were washed ashore in Fécamp and a pilgrimage still takes place today as a mark of devotion. The abbey was overrun by the Vikings (the nuns disfigured themselves before the invader's eyes prior to being martyred) but was rebuilt in 932 and dedicated to the Holy Trinity. In the 11th century, Duke Richard II made it a monastery, a place of pilgrimage and an authoritative spiritual and cultural centre under the guidance of its abbot, William de Volpiano. Its sphere of influence was immense, and was to last right up to the French Revolution.

Holy Trinity Church is the largest remnant of the abbey, along with the Town Hall which is housed in the former monastic buildings. Built between 1175 and 1220 to replace the Romanesque construction, it is a fine example of Early Norman Gothic architecture ; indeed, its grandeur and size set it on an equal footing with the most famous cathedrals. A tall lantern-tower, a common feature of Norman architecture, rises above the transept crossing. The façade was refurbished in the 18th century in the Classical style.

The long **nave** flanked by galleries leads to a vast **chancel** containing a large number of side chapels. Among the tombs in the chapels are those of Dukes Richard I and II, both patrons of the church, and Abbot William Volpiano. The Renaissance brought to the church a series of masterpieces like the sculpted screens separating the chapels and aisle, which were made at the beginning of the 16th century thanks to Abbot A. Bohier. A realistic sculpture representing the Dormition of the Virgin Mary (c. 1495) decorates the right hand crossing, which also contains the reliquary known as the 'Angel's Footstep'. It is said that the footprint in the stone belongs to an angel who descended from heaven on the day the new monastery was to be consecrated, in the 10th century, to insist that it be dedicated to the Holy Trinity. Behind the High Altar, with its 18th century canopy, is a Renaissance altar decorated with bas-reliefs, the work of an Italian craftsman, Girolano Viscardo. He also created the Tabernacle of the Precious Blood which is in the Flamboyant Lady Chapel.

The **Benedictine Distillery** is housed in a 19th century Gothic and Renaissance-style building. It was in the 16th century that Brother Vincelli had the idea of distilling aromatic plants from along the cliff tops in a mixture of cognac and armagnac. Le Grand rediscovered the famous liqueur in the 19th century and its reputation spread further afield. The **museum** houses the collections of this industrialist and patron of the Arts.

Fécamp is a bustling port with an important timber trade, but it also has facilities for sailing buffs. As far back and the 16th century, fleets set sail to fish cod off Iceland and Newfoundland. The Newfoundland fishermen were away at sea for several month at a time, living and working in very difficult conditions. The industry has since been modernised and has been extended to include canning, salting, and the wet fish trade.

From the top of the 350 ft. North Cliff (falaise Nord), the tallest along the Normandy coast, on which stands the **Chapel of Our Lady of Salvation** (Notre-Dame-du-Salut), a place of pilgrimage for seafarers, there is a view over the harbour, the town and the coastline as far as Etretat.

It is said that Guy de Maupassant was born in Fécamp, although his birth was registered at Miromesnil Town Hall.

To the south of Fécamp lies **Bailleul Castle,** set in extensive grounds. Its richly-decorated Renaissance façades, which are particularly ornate at roof level, are in sharp contrast to the building's rather plain side walls. The castle is lavishly-furnished.

FLERS (Orne)
25 miles W. of Argentan.

Flers is situated in the wooded area of the Bocage, and three-quarters of the town was

Rouen : *the façade of the Law Courts.*

Ô : *the castle.*

destroyed in June 1944. It has been the centre of the cotton industry for the past one hundred years and has now branched out into electronics.

The L-shaped **castle** beside a lake, still has one wing dating from the 16th century although it has undergone much alteration since then. It was the work of the alchemist, Nicholas Grosparmy. The main façade is Classical in design. During the French Revolution, it was the headquarters of the Chouan rebels ; today, it is a museum.

To the west of Flers, the small town of **Tinchebray,** now the centre of iron-smelting, keeps alive the memory of the famous victory in 1106 of King Henry I of England over his brother, Robert Curthose, who thereby lost the Duchy of Normandy. It is the home town of the surrealist writer, André Breton.

Mount Cerisi rises between the rivers Vère and Noireau. A path lined with rhodedendron bushes leads to the summit from which there is a panoramic view over the Bocage and the Norman Alps.

FONTAINE-HENRY (Calvados)

6 miles from Caen.

The castle of Fontaine-Henry stands in the fertile Mue Valley. Originally the home of the Tilly family (Henry de Tilly gave his name to the village), it later became the property of the Harcourts.

Built on the site of a mediaeval fortress, of which the vaulted cellars and chapel (refurbished in the 16th century) still remain, the graceful building we see today was completed in the 15th and 16th centuries. The decoration of the irregular façades sums up the various architectural styles which came into fashion between the reigns of Charles VIII and Henri II. The influence of the Italian Renaissance is manifest in the fantastic combination of arabesques, medallions, and projecting or overlying columns, all of which seem to be superimposed onto a piece of architecture that is still resolutely Gothic.

One wing of the building, which was completed in 1537 and decorated in part by Le Prestre, is distinctive because of its immense sloping roof and its enormous chimney. The roof is, in fact, taller than the walls of the building itself. The façade of the main part of the castle is a masterpiece of intricate sculpture, a sort of lacework in stone. Inside the castle, is a collection of furniture and Old Masters built up over the years by successive generations.

GAILLON (Eure)

15 miles N.E. of Evreux.

Built on a site with an excellent view of the Seine Valley, the fortress gifted to the Archbishop of Rouen by Saint Louis was converted c. 1500 by Georges I of Amboise, himself one of Louis XII's ministers, into a sumptuous Renaissance castle resembling an Italian palace. The art treasures accumulated by the prelate made the building a monument of avant-garde architectural design and contributed to the launching in Normandy of this hitherto unknown style.

Famous architects, including Pierre Fain, sculptors such as Michel Colombe, Jean Juste and Laurent Mugiano, (some of whose works have been removed to the Louvre) all helped to produce the elegance and opulence for which the castle was renowned. In Louis XIV's reign, it was further embellished and enlarged by Hardouin-Mansart, while Le Nôtre was responsible for landscaping the garden.

Ransacked during the French Revolution, before becoming a prison, barracks and finally a factory, the 'Renaissance Versailles' is now being renovated under the aegis of the French equivalent of the Arts Council.

On both sides of the **gate-house**, the decoration is both graceful and unusual : the carvings on the pilasters represent foliage* and shells, and are characteristic of the early French Renaissance. Between the two large towers which once housed the chapel and the cardinal's room, the gallery and the turreted staircase decorated with medallions are all that remain of the **castle** whose riches have been scattered far and wide.

GRANVILLE (Manche)

15 miles N.W. of Avranches.

Like the adjoining Bay of the Mont Saint-Michel, the seaside resort of Granville has the strongest tides in Europe. Its climate is invigorating ; what more suitable place, then, for a

Honfleur : *Saint-Catherine's quay.* ▶

thalassotherapy centre. In addition to its bustling yacht harbour, there is a busy commercial port in the town, and inshore fishing is an important industry. Every year, the summer brings the Procession (or 'Pardon') of the Guilds and the Sea. There are daily ferry links with Chausey and the Channel Islands.

The Upper Town, with its old houses of granite reminding the visitor that Brittany is not far away, was built within the ramparts on top of Granville Rock, a promontory which is connected to the mainland by a narrow isthmus. The English cut the settlement off in the 15th century by digging a moat known as the 'Englishmen's Trench', and undertook the building of fortifications, but the town are recaptured shortly afterwards by Captain d'Estouteville. The Lower Town was developed on land reclaimed from the sea.

The town was later attacked several times during the various wars with the English and, in the 18th century, it resisted assault by the rebels from the Vendée and gained itself the name 'Granville-la-Victoire'. Its privateers and seafarers distinguished themselves on several occasions. The 1939-45 war has left behind vestiges of the "Atlantic Wall".

A walk along the ramparts enables the visitor to look seawards to the Isles Chausey and, in fine weather, as far as the coast of Brittany. Near the beach, the **Christian Dior Gardens** are a reminder that the great fashion designer was born in Granville, as was the painter Maurice Denis.

In the wooded undulating Thar Valley between Avranches and Granville, are the ruins of **La Lucerne d'Outre-Mer Abbey** which have undergone extensive restoration since 1959. Founded for the Premonstratensian Order by Hasculfe de Subligny, great-nephew of William the Conqueror, it was ravaged by war, rebuilt in the 17th century by Jean de La Bellière, and turned into a cotton mill during the French Revolution.

The Cistercian influence is obvious in the Romanesque-Gothic **church** layout, and the building is again being used for its original purpose. The 18th century cloisters have disappeared except for the north-west corner near a Romanesque lavatorium. A mediaeval dovecot stands next to the Classical abbey buildings. Exhibitions are now held in the former monastic rooms.

The elegant 16th century Renaissance castle of **Chanteloup,** built by Antoine d'Estouteville, forms a striking contrast to the two mediaeval towers of an older building. The work has occasionally been attributed to H. Sohier, the architect of Saint Peter's Church in Caen.

Not far from **Mount Robin** with its panoramic view of the Bocage region, the impressive ruins of the Benedictine Abbey of **Hambye** are a fine example of Early Norman Gothic architecture. The abbey was established in the valley of the R. Seine in 1145 by William Paynel, and the ogival, or pointed, arch is an indication of the beginnings of Gothic architecture in Normandy.

Because there are no side aisles in the Romanesque **abbey church,** its overall height seems greater than it actually is. The lantern-tower, which was opened up in the 19th century, and the 13th century Gothic chancel are unusually spacious. In the chancel, experts have discovered flagstones marking the graves of Jeanne Paynel, a descendant of the Abbey's founder, and her husband Louis d'Estouteville who was governor of the Mont Saint-Michel.

The buildings which have been restored give the visitor some idea of the life of the monks. They are the 15th century chaptel house, the Hall of the Deceased. which is decorated with frescoes, the warming-room, and the farm outbuildings.

HAVRE (LE) (Seine-Maritime)
127 miles N.W. of Paris and 53 miles N.W. of Rouen.

Almost entirely flattened at the time of the Liberation, when there were one hundred and forty-six air raids in succession, the urban community of Le Havre was redeveloped by Perret, a town planner who paid particular attention to uniformity of design. The town, which is very well-situated at the intersection of the R. Seine and one of the busiest seas in the world, has the second largest commercial harbour in France (after Marseilles) and this has ensured the city's development particularly in the fields of metalwork, ship-repairing, timber, cotton, and oil with its by-products.

It was in 1517 that François I decided on the construction of a fortified "Safe Haven" to replace the ports of Harfleur and Honfleur which were silting up. High tide in Le Havre lasted for two hours, which was a distinct advantage for any harbour with a future in the seafaring world. Gradually, the town spread beyond the cliff top (Ingouville) and development started up the hill.

Le Havre boasts many famous sons and daughters : the writers Georges and Madeleine de Scudéry, Bernardin de Saint-Pierre, Casimir Delavigne and R. Queneau, the composer A. Honegger, and the painters O. Friesz and R. Dufy. Here, too, Monet started his career as a caricaturist and met his teacher, Boudin, who himself felt deeply attached to the town although he was not, in fact, born there. It was also the birthplace of the economist and socio-logist, André Siegfried.

Entirely rebuilt after 1945, the town has nevertheless retained the chequered layout first established in the 16th century, although the streets are now wider and gardens and open spaces have been contrived between the austere, ordered buildings that are reminiscent of Classical architecture. Auguste Perret, the "Father of Reinforced Concrete", has left his mark on the town's main public buildings : rhythm in the forms used, well-balanced volume, and overall unity. A striking example of his work is the spacious **Town Hall Square** (Place de l'Hôtel de Ville). At the end of the Avenue Foch, a majestic thoroughfare leading to the sea not far from the yacht basin, stands the Ocean Gateway (Porte Océane) flanked by two tall towers, symbolising the welcome extented to travellers and the town's vocation as an outgoing international port with a large back-up network of communications.

Saint Joseph's Church, built of bare concrete, has a lantern-tower some 350 ft. high. The square interior is rendered particularly impressive by the building materials used, the lighting and the overall height. Beams of light filter into the church through thousands of pieces of coloured glass, changing in intensity as the day wears on.

The unusual glass and metal structure that is the **André Malraux Museum of Fine Arts** (Musée des Beaux-Arts) stands out near the harbour. Thanks to several bequests, it now houses a fine collection of works from the Pre-Impressionist period up to the present day, and has a large number of paintings by Boudin and Dufy.

The harbour owes its wealth to the French East India Company and to the help given to the rebels during the American War of Independance. The first steam-powered transatlantic liner was launched in 1864. There are sixteen miles of wharves connecting dozens of basins (covering a total area of 3 sq. miles), huge warehouses, and three terminals handling goods and passengers (there are numerous ferry services to England and Ireland). Ships pass through the François I lock, the biggest in the world, on their way upstream to the industrial estate. Visitors can watch them from the jetty below the signal-station, or take a boat trip round the docks.

The oil terminal of **Havre-Antifer,** which has recently been rebuilt along the coast towards Etretat, can handle giant supertankers.

From **Ingouville Hill** (Côte d'Ingouville), there is a view over the industrial estate and the harbour. Further to the north-west, the old village of **Sainte-Adresse,** situated on the floor of a river valley, has become a residential area with its own seaside resort. From the **fort,** one can see the whole city and the Calvados coast. There is yet another, quite different, view from **La Hève Cape.**

Saint Honorine's abbey church, Romanesque in style, was built in **Graville** at the end of the 11th century on the site of a sanctuary which housed the relics of the saint whose body had

Saint-Gabriel-Brécy : *the old priory.*

Saint-Martin-de-Boscherville : *façade of the abbey church of Saint-Georges-de-Boscherville.* ▶

been washed ashore there after being thrown into the R. Seine. The relics were taken to Conflans when the Vikings arrived, but the church still contains the miraculous sarcophagus that dates from the 4th century. The decorated capitals in the nave are a naive interpretation of orientally-inspired designs. In the 13th and 17th century monastic buildings is the **Priory Museum.**

Once a seaport, **Harfleur** has become an industrial suburb of Le Havre since the estuary started to silt up. The Flamboyant **Saint Martin's Church** has a tall stone bell-tower built in the 15th century.

HONFLEUR (Calvados)
21 miles N. of Lisieux.

Synonymous with charm and poetry, this lively little port on the left bank of the Seine Estuary opposite Le Havre remains unaltered by modern trends. It has an inestimable historical and artistic atmosphere into which the visitor is plunged as he wanders through the old streets.

The town existed far back in time but owes its development to the fortifications ordered by Charles V in the 14th century, and its military importance during the One Hundred Year's

100

War. In the 15th century, ship-building became a growth industry, while the great voyages of discovery undertaken a century later reflected honour on local shipowners and seafarers alike. It was from here that Paulmier de Gonneville set off to discover Brazil, which he reached in 1503, that Jean Denis set sail for the New World, discovering Newfoundland and the Saint Lawrence Seaway in 1506. Later, Champlain landed in Canada and founded Quebec (1608) where Normand settlers established a colony.

Despite fierce competition from Le Havre, business flourished and cod-fishing gained in importance. In the 17th century, Colbert ordered the harbour installations of the Old Basin (Vieux Bassin), and the building of salterns, two of which are still in existence today. After the deeply-felt loss of Canada and the troubled period of the French Revolution, Honfleur found a new source of wealth in the 19th century — timber importing, a trade which is still thriving to this very day. The town also began to attract artists who were fascinated by its contrasting colours, the reflections of the harbour, and the distinctive atmosphere of the place.

Isabey de Jongkind came to Honfleur as early as 1824. Boudin often revisited his native town. He was at the centre of the 'Saint Simeon' school of painting which derived its name from Old Mother Toutain's inn where meetings were held, attended by Baudelaire and Monet. These meetings were to give rise to Impressionism. The town was also the birthplace of historian Albert Sorel, the composer E. Satie, and his friends the humourist A. Allais, whose father's chemist's shop, called "Passocéan" (a remedy for seasickness !), still exists. The poets H. de Régnier and Lucie Delarue-Mardrus came from Honfleur. Indeed, the town has made a considerable contribution to modern art, and present-day painters continue to congregate here.

In addition to the small fishing fleet and its shipyards, Honfleur is the centre of a flourishing timber trade. A yachting marina has been established in the **Old Basin** which was originally built by Duquesne on Colbert's orders. Iridescent images are reflected in its water, blurred pictures of a compact row of attractive houses with slate roofs. Space was at a premium, so the houses spread upwards rather than outwards. Opposite Saint Catherine's Quay is Saint Stephen's Quay, which was once part of the 'Enclosure'. The oldest church in Honfleur, Saint Stephen's (église Saint-Etienne), has become a **Museum** of Seafaring and Local Lore (musée de la Marine and musée folklorique).

Saint Catherine's Church is an unusual building. Made entirely of wood, except for the foundations, it was erected after the English occupation during the One Hundred Years' War. As qualified architects were busy with more extensive rebuilding programmes, the church was constructed by ships' joiners using wood from the Touques Forest (end-15th and 16th centuries). The twin naves in the shape of upturned hulls rest on wooden pillars. Wood was also used for the sculpting of the church's statues. Saint Catherine's bell-tower, with its weatherboarding* and props which give it a curious shape, was purposefully built apart from the church itself. It originally provided accomadation for the bell-ringer.

The **Eugène-Boudin Museum** is almost entirely given over to the work of local artists from the pre-Impressionist period to the present day. The best-known of these painters is, of course, Boudin himself.

From the **Coast of Grace** (Côte de Grâce) dotted with apple trees, there is a panoramic view of the estuary and Le Havre. An elegant Renaissance chapel to **Our Lady of Grace** is the scene of the Sailor's Pilgrimage every year at Whitsun. The nearby **Saint Simeon's Farm** has become a hotel.

HOULGATE (Calvados)
22 miles N.W. of Lisieux.

This bustling seaside resort lies in the cool Drochon river valley above a vast sandbank where shrimpers abound at low tide. From the observation platform at the tope of the Houlgate Hill (Butte d'Houlgate), there is a fine view of the Floral Coast.

Towards Villiers, the old marl and clay geological formation known as the Auberville Plateau plunges down to the sea at the spot called the **Black Cow Cliffs** (Falaises des Vaches Noires). These are strange high cliffs, and rockfalls are fairly commonplace. On the shore below, collectors find large amounts of minerals and fossils at low tide. In the place known as the **'Chaos'**, where the fallen rocks and scree are covered with dark seaweed, enthusiasts have even found the fossils of large prehistoric vertebrates.

JUBLAINS (Mayenne)
6 miles S.E. of Mayenne.

To the south-east of Mayenne, the Gallo-Roman fortifications of Jublains (once known as Noviodunum) are the finest example of such early remains in Normandy (3rd. century). Several roads met in this trading post, for the entire road network between Brittany and the Cherbourg Peninsula converged on this point.

Roman baths are distinguishable within the walls.

JUMIEGES (Seine-Maritime)
17 miles W. of Rouen.

On a site near the forest enclosed by a meander of the R. Seine stand the ruins of the Benedictine abbey of Jumièges, a grandiose stone building which still conveys something of the mysticism, austerity and ambition of its creators.

The monastery was founded in 654 by Saint Philibert, courtisan to the King, who suddenly decided to offer his life to God. Ransacked by the Vikings, it was restored early in the 11th century by William Longsword and nicknamed "Jumièges the Almoner" because of the charity extended by its monks. The Duke had promised to undertake its reconstruction after a hunting accident in Jumièges Forest when he was almost killed by a wild boar.

The zeal of William de Volpiano, who was supported by Richard II, contributed to the abbey's prosperity and made it one of the richest communities in Normandy. Moreover, it entertained excellent relations with the kings of France. Its cultural and religious influence was far-reaching and the reputation gained by its teaching attracted many philosophers. Its decline began in the 18th century and the French Revolution finally destroyed the buildings which were used as a barracks before becoming a quarry. An industrialist blew up the tower.

Notre Dame abbey church was consecrated in 1067 by Archbishop Maurville of Rouen in the presence of William the Conqueror. Its huge façade, composed of a forepart (a veritable porch which is a remnant of Carolingian architecture) flanked by two tall towers, is a precursor of the 'harmonic Norman façade' as apparent in Caen where the forepart has disappeared. Behind the façade, is a wide gallery opening onto the nave, which is an elongated structure with no beams. The alternating pillars and columns are its most striking feature. Galleries above the side aisles were once connected to those in the transept which is now in a very bad state of repair. A large arch still supports one of the walls of the lantern-tower. Despite monastic enclosure, the Romanesque chancel includes an ambulatory. It was replaced in the 13th century by a Gothic chancel of which only two radiating chapels remain.

'Charles VII's Passage', thus named in memory of the monarch who had come to see Agnès Sorel in Mesnil-sous-Jumièges, leads to **Saint Peter's Church.** It bears witness to architectural experimentation in the 10th century, for its porch and the first few bays of the nave are Pre-Romanesque and Carolingien. The remainder of the building is 13th and 14th century.

The early-12th century **chapter house** used to open onto cloisters, which no longer exist, bounded by a large cellar comprising several rooms.

In the 17th century accommodation block, is a museum of sculpture. Two 14th century recumbent figures are reminders of the legend of the Unnerved of Jumièges : the sons of Clovis II, who had rebelled against their mother Batilda, were subjected to torture by unnerving

Lisors : *the ruins of Mortemer abbey.*

(i.e. the burning of the hamstring). They were then cast adrift in a boat on the Seine. Given shelter in Jumièges by Saint Philibert, they died shortly afterwards.

LESSAY (Manche)
13 miles N. of Coutances

The village of Lessay lies in the narrowest part of the Cherbourg Peninsula, between the Gorges Marshes in the east and the Ay Estuary in the west. Nearby is the vast moorland mentioned in Barbey d'Aurevilly's book "The Bewitched Woman", but it is now losing something of its atmosphere of desolation. The church in Lessay, a perfect example of Romanesque architecture, was exceptionally well-restored after being damaged by a mine in 1944.

The charter setting up the monastery mentions 'Exaquium' ('reclaimed land') which later became 'L'Exat', then 'Lessay'. **Holy Trinity Abbey,** which was founded for Benedictines from the Bec Monastery in the 11th century by the lord of **La Haye-du-Puits,** Richard Turstin Haldup, was influential throughout the Cherbourg Peninsula and, indeed, in England.

The austere lines of the former **minster,** now the parish church, highlight the harmony and severity of its early Romanesque style. The roof and 12th century square bell-tower are built of schist from La Hague.

Uniformity and simplicity are again in evidence inside the church ; the Benedictine layout has been strictly adhered to. Apse, chancel and transept are 11th century, the nave late-11th — early-12th century. It comprises some of the earliest examples of the pointed Norman arch. A clerestory passage runs round the building within the walls themselves, and the

104

Mont Saint-Michel : *the lace staircase.*

modern stained glass windows with designs based on Irish manuscripts, introduce a soft lighting effect particularly conducive to meditation.

In the middle of September every year, the **Millenial Holy Cross Fair** takes place on the adjacent moorland. It is a horse fair, dog show, and colourful fête. It is a picturesque event, and the most characteristic of its kind in Normandy. In his book, "Mon Vieux Lessay", Desdevises du Dezet says it can be heard "roaring like the tide at the equinoxes".

LILLEBONNE (Seine-Maritime)
23 miles E. of Le Havre.

The capital of the Caletae, or people of the Caux Region, lies to the north of the Seine Estuary. Named Juliabona by the Romans in honour of Julius Caesar, it was later fortified by William the Conqueror.

In this small industrial town, there are the ruins of a vast semi-elliptical **theatre** dating back to Antiquity. Its original layout is still discernible (it is 350 ft. long). Of William the Conqueror's **castle,** which was rebuilt in the 12th and 13th centuries by the Counts of Harcourt, only the ruins of a cylindrical keep are still standing.

LISIEUX (Calvados)
31 miles E. of Caen.

This is the capital of the rich fertile Auge Region. Lying in the Touques Valley, where apple orchards abound, the former bishopric is now a busy agricultural town and the centre of a number of different industries. It is also a place of pilgrimage (early October).

Although Thérèse Martin was born in Alençon in 1873, it was in Lisieux that she spent her childhood, in the Buissonnets House where she came to live on her mother's death. At the age of nine, she had already decided that she wished to become a Carmelite ; six years later, she received special dispensation from Pope Leo XIII. She died at the age of 24, after reaching the very peak of mysticism and spirituality.

During the Liberation, the town was badly damaged by fire. In particular, almost the entire district of old Gothic houses was destroyed ; only a few buildings survived. The old town is conjured up by the exhibition in the Museum which bears its name (**Musée du Vieux Lisieux).**

Saint Peter's Cathedral was left standing. Built in the 12th and 13th centuries, it has a flight of steps leading up to the main façade, which is flanked by two towers. The one on the right was rebuilt in the 16th century in the Romanesque style ; the other dates from the 13th century and is very ornate. The Paradise Doorway leads into the south crossing. The interior reflects the austerity of the Early Gothic style of architecture, while the nave is reminiscent of its counterparts in the Paris Basin. Sculpted reliefs and 13th century stained glass decorate the south transept. In the apsidal chapel (where Saint Thérèse used to attend Mass), rebuilt in the Flamboyant style by Bishop Pierre Couchon of Lisieux, is the prelate's own tomb. He was among those who voted for the death sentence at Joan of Arc's trial.

The gilded chamber in the former **Bishop's Palace** adjacent to the cathedral has a highly-ornate coffered* ceiling.

Shortly after the canonisation of Sister Teresa of the Child Jesus in 1925, work began on the grandiose **Saint Teresa's Basilica** (1929). It was consecrated in 1954 but its architectural style did not meet with universal approval. Its dome is over 300 ft. high, and both exterior and interior were designed with an eye to realism. The crypt, which is decorated with mosaics, has space for four thousand pilgrims.

A son et lumière in the summer months and a diorama near the Convent complete the town's portrait of the saint.

In **Crèvecœur-en-Auge,** the **Schlumberger Museum** is devoted to developments in the search for oil and to the inventions of the two brothers, both engineers.

For some time, they lived in the former **abbey of Val-Richer** which is situated in a deep valley. The Cistercian house was founded in 1167 by a monk from Clairvaux and Thomas à Becket sought refuge there for a while. It underwent restoration in the 17th century but was again altered by François Guizot, minister to Louis-Philippe, who wrote his historical works in the castle and who died there in 1874.

Nearby is **La Roque-Baignard,** a 15th-16h century **castle** which once belonged to the historian Labbey de la Roque and which was a favourite with the writer André Gide. It appears in his novel "The Immoralist" under the name "La Morinière".

LOUVIERS (Eure)
18 miles S.E. of Rouen.

Situated in a wooded region, the old draper's town of Louviers on the banks of the R. Eure (known in the Middle Ages as 'Locus Veri' or 'Place of Springtime' because of its fertile environment), is now a centre of electrical engineering and electronics. The cloth industry, which was flourishing as far back as the 13th century, received much encouragement from Colbert when the town became the main supplier of the French Court. It went into a serious decline at the time of the French Revolution.

The Gothic **Church of Our Lady** (Notre-Dame), begun in the 13th century, is now as big as a cathedral, having been enlarged and altered in the 15th and 16th centuries. The Flamboyant style can be see at its most ornate in the royal porch. The delicately-sculpted pinnacles* and openwork balustrade on the south wall form a striking contrast to the plainness of the west front. The nave, with its double side-aisles, is decorated with sculpted panels and statues, some of which come from the castle of Gaillon. One of the Renaissance windows illustrates a procession in which the guilds of drapers are taking part.

None of the locals could tell us whether the words of the old song were still true today : "On the road to Louviers (repeat)... can be seen a roadmender (repeat)... He daily breaks up stones with which he'll (repeat)... pave the way for the carriage wheel (repeat)."

Upstream stands **Acquigny** castle. Renaissance façades frame a turret which serves as a squinch*.

LYONS (FOREST OF)
12 miles N.E. of Les Andelys.

The State-owned **Forest of Lyons,** generally considered to be one of the finest beech woods in France, is composed of a number of thickets planted with enormous trees most of which are over 65 ft. high. The Bunodière Beech tops 135 ft.

On the banks of the R. Fouillebroc, only the ruins of the vast 12th century church belonging to the Cistercian **abbey of Mortemer** still exist today. In one of its walls, there is a funereal niche. Of the monastery buildings, all that remains is the wall of the chapter house with the dormitory above, the gatehouse, and a dovecot. One building dating from the Classical period is still lived in.

La Forestière castle is situated in the midst of extensive grounds near the confluence of the rivers Andelle and Crevon, in **Vascœuil.** It was here that Michelet wrote part of his "History of France". Now it is an international cultural and exhibition centre.

It is said that Flaubert based Yonville-l'Abbaye in "Madame Bovary" on the real-life village of **Ry,** which lies on the R. Crevon. Moreover, Emma is said to share some traits of character with Delphine Couturier, the wife of Dr. Delamare. A collection of mechanical figures retelling parts of the story of the famous novel are displayed in the Bovary Gallery. Entry to the **Church of Saint-Sulpice** (12th-16th century) is by way of a carved wooden porch dating

Mont Saint-Michel : *seen from the west.*

from the Renaissance. The late Gothic **Martainville Castle,** whose large chimneys are examples of decorative brickwork, is the home of the 'Rural Folk Museum of Upper Normandy'

MONDAYE (Calvados)
South of Bayeux.

The church and monastery of Mondaye to the south of Bayeux, which are still in use today, are outstanding examples of Classical architecture.

The Premonstratensian Abbey of Saint Martin was founded in 1212 and rebuilt from 1706-1743 by Father Eustace Restout, the uncle of the celebrated artist who carried out the pictorial decoration of the **church.** The building is of graceful proportions. The gigantic organ case was sculpted by Melchior Verly, as was the terracotta statue of the Assumption.

To Canadians and British people, the abbey has become the spiritual memorial to those who lost their lives during the Normandy Campaign of 1944.

MONT SAINT-MICHEL (Manche)
14 miles S.W. of Avranches.

Jutting out from the Bay which stretches from Cancale to Granville is the Mont Saint-Michel, a rocky island almost half-a-mile in circumference connected to the mainland by a causeway built in 1879. A prominent place of pilgrimage (it celebrated its millenium in 1966),

108

Mont Saint-Michel : *the Knight's Room.*

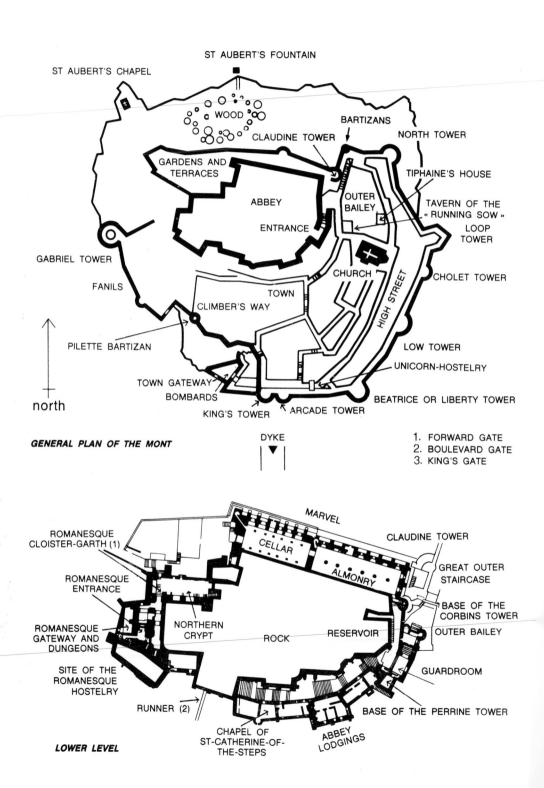

ST AUBERT'S FOUNTAIN

ST AUBERT'S CHAPEL

WOOD

BARTIZANS

CLAUDINE TOWER

NORTH TOWER

TIPHAINE'S HOUSE

GARDENS AND
TERRACES

TAVERN OF THE
« RUNNING SOW »

OUTER
BAILEY

LOOP
TOWER

ABBEY

ENTRANCE

CHOLET TOWER

GABRIEL TOWER

CHURCH

HIGH STREET

FANILS

TOWN

CLIMBER'S WAY

LOW TOWER

PILETTE BARTIZAN

UNICORN-HOSTELRY

TOWN GATEWAY

BOMBARDS

BEATRICE OR LIBERTY TOWER

north

KING'S TOWER

ARCADE TOWER

GENERAL PLAN OF THE MONT

DYKE

1. FORWARD GATE
2. BOULEVARD GATE
3. KING'S GATE

MARVEL

ROMANESQUE
CLOISTER-GARTH (1)

CELLAR

CLAUDINE TOWER

ALMONRY

GREAT OUTER
STAIRCASE

ROMANESQUE
ENTRANCE

BASE OF THE
CORBINS TOWER

ROMANESQUE
GATEWAY AND
DUNGEONS

NORTHERN
CRYPT

ROCK

RESERVOIR

OUTER BAILEY

SITE OF THE
ROMANESQUE
HOSTELRY

GUARDROOM

RUNNER (2)

BASE OF THE PERRINE TOWER

CHAPEL OF
ST-CATHERINE-OF-
THE-STEPS

ABBEY
LODGINGS

LOWER LEVEL

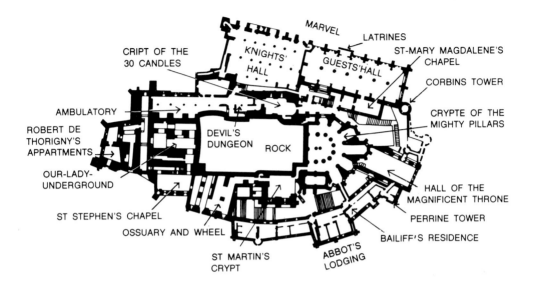

INTERMEDIATE LEVEL

THE MONT SAINT-MICHEL : GENERAL PLAN AND PLANS OF THE VARIOUS STOREYS OF THE ABBEY

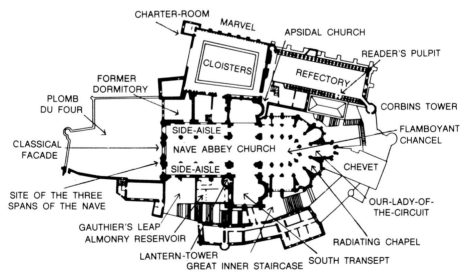

UPPER LEVEL, CHURCH

111

Mont Saint-Michel : *the cloisters in the 'Marvel'.*

the abbey-fortress is an extraordinary combination of architectural styles, all adapted to the needs of this particular site.

The Mont is surrounded by vast grey mudflats and the gentleness of their slope causes a spectacular phenomenon to take place, expecially at the equinoxes. Because the tides are very high at that time, the sea rushes in very fast, occasionally trapping fishermen or unwary tourists out walking on the sandbanks (once waterlogged, the sandbanks are 'mobile' and dangerous, in fact they become 'quicksands'). "When the sea was within our sight, it took on the appearance of a cavalry charge led by white horses..." (T. Gautier's "Excursion to the Mont Saint-Michel" in the paper "Le Moniteur" in April 1860). Progressive silting-up of the bay caused by embankment and drainage projects has decreased the rate at which the water rises at high tide, except in exceptional circumstances. The saltings, fertile meadows reclaimed from the sea over the last century, are ideal sheep grazing land. Three rivers flow into the bay, the Sée, the Sélune and the Couesnon which forms the boundary between Brittany and Normandy.

> *"The Couesnon has, in its folly,*
>
> *Put the Mount in Normandy."*

Originally, Mont Tombe, later the Mont Saint-Michel, was a rock approximately 280 ft. high overlooking the vast Forest of Scissy, as were Mount Tombella (Tombelaine) and Mount Dol. Christian hermits lived in the forest in the Merovingian era. Legend has it that, when they were hungry, the hermits on the Mount would light a beacon and its smoke let a priest in

Mont Saint-Michel : *the Northern crypt.*

Astériac (Beauvoir) know of their needs ; he would then load provisions onto his donkey and send it off alone through the woods. One day, the unfortunate animal was eaten by a wolf, but an invisible force made the carnivore transport the provisions to Mount Tombe. Henceforth, it was the wolf from Astériac which acted as messenger boy.

In 709, a tidal wave swamped the forest and isolated the Mont. That same year, the archangel Michael appeared three times to Bishop Aubert of Avranches and ordered him to build an oratory. Faced with Aubert's disbelief, Michael is said to have poked his finger into the bishop's forehead.

The cult of Saint Michael, patron saint of Normandy, came from the East. He had already appeared several times in Italy, in Monte Gargano and Rome (San Angelo) and was venerated both for his rôle as warmonger and prince of the heavenly host, and as arbiter and weigher of souls. And so Aubert built an oratory on a site which was known to be a place of miracles, for a stolen bull had been found at the very top of the rock and, moreover, the morning dew had marked out the circumference of the area required for the building's foundations. Aubert established a small community and had sacred relics brought from Italy. The Mont was dedicated to Saint Michael.

Obviously it was quite common for monks to found communities on uninhabited islands or high up in the mountains where they were far removed from crowds and earthly pleasures.

The Mount-of-Saint-Michael-in-peril-from-the-sea rapidly became a much-frequented place of pilgrimage. From 840 onwards, Viking invasions threatened the coastal settlements and their inhabitants sought refuge with the monks, thereby establishing the first village on the rock. In 965, Duke Richard I of Normandy replaced the community with Benedictine monks from Fontanelle under the guidance of Mainard. The Abbey was founded ; the church of Our-Lady-Underground is the earliest part of the building. At the beginning of the 11th century, Duke Richard II and William de Volpiano, the monk from Lombardy (cf. Fécamp), decided on the construction of a Romanesque monastery.

As the Abbey's intellectual influence spread, so it acquired more and more land along the coast ; William the Conqueror even granted it fiefs in England. All this material wealth was gifted by pilgrims, welldoers and patrons. Early on in the Abbey's life, important people came to beg for the archangel's assistance. And Richard II donated a great deal of property to the Mont on the occasion of his marriage to Judith of Brittany which was celebrated here.

The Abbey reached the peak of its prosperity in the 12th century and, with it, came widespread religious and cultural influence. Henry II Plantagenet, one of the Western world's most powerful monarchs, took as his counsellor the Abbot of the Mont Saint-Michel, Robert de Torigni, a man of excellent taste and a skilful administrator. He it was who built up a rich library of illuminated manuscripts and created the 'city of books' where Guillaume de Saint-Pair wrote his "Story of Mont Saint-Michel".

In 1204, one of Philippe Auguste's allies set fire to a part of the Mont in order to recapture it from the Dukes of Normandy. With the compensation paid by the French king, the then Abbot, Raoul des Iles, began the building of the "Marvel", a masterpiece of Gothic architecture which was to be continued by Richard Turstin. The life of the community was punctuated by processions, and grand ceremonials on the occasion of Royal Visits. From the 14th to the 18th centuries, groups of children from all corners of Europe set out on pilgrimages which were known as the "Marches of the Little Shepherds" : the young people left behind family and homeland, sometimes for many months, in order to carry their standards to Saint Michael.

War seemed imminent at the beginning of the 14th century and the Abbey was fortified. Pierre Le Roi built the outer bailey and barbican, and completed work on the Abbot's apartments. After winning the Battle of Agincourt in 1415, the English recaptured Normandy but, although the monks were betrayed by their Superior, Robert Jolivet, they resisted all attacks under the leadership of Captain Louis d'Estouteville. For a long time, this was the only French victory. Devotion to Saint Michael (which was encouraged by Joan of Arc) became stronger than ever.

In 1469, Louis XI instituted the Order of Chivalry of Saint Michael. He also had one of his "daughters" set up on the Mont : a wooden and iron cage suspended from the dungeon ceiling in which prisoners swung incessantly back and forth in icy solitude. In the 16th century, during the Wars of Religion, the Abbey was besieged several times.

The community's code of ethics had become increasingly lax over the years, especially since the introduction of the commendatory system which allowed a non-resident Abbot to draw revenue from the monastery. Finally, in 1622, the monks were replaced by Maurists, a reformed congregation of the Benedictine order, who were to remain on the Mont until the

114

French Revolution.

The Abbey then became a prison. Common law offenders and political prisoners were incarcerated in dreadfully unhygienic conditions. At the time of the Convention, the Mont acquired a somewhat paradoxical new name, Mount Freedom. Personnalities from all walks of life protested against the abusive use of the Abbey, among them Hugo, Chateaubriand and Viollet-le-Duc, but the prison was not closed until 1863, during the reign of Napoleon III. The Ancient Monuments began restoration work in 1874. Now, a small number of monks again occupy the Abbey, which has thereby regained its original function. It is once more a sanctuary, a place of prayer and devotion.

A famous pilgrimage takes place every year for Michaelmas (on the nearest Sunday to September 29th) and the saint is also honoured in May.

The traveller arriving at the Mont Saint-Michel cannot but be astonished at its originality, the result of the successful fulfilment of three requirements : prayer (for it is the House of God), hospitality for visiting pilgrims, and, lastly, defence since the very fact of its insularity has given its military, as well as religious, importance.

The visitor passes the outer wall by way of the **Forward Gate** (Porte de l'Avancée) to the left of the Arcade and King's Towers. The entrance dates from 1530. In the first courtyard, there are two bombards captured from the English and known as the 'Michelettes'. The second courtyard, which contains Old Mother Poulard's Hotel famous for its omelettes (in which cream and the whipped-up egg whites are added to the beaten yolks), leads to the **King's Gate** (Porte du Roi). Above it, are the King's apartments. The gate was built by Jolivet at the beginning of the 15th century and, at that time, there was a drawbridge across the outer moat. The arms of the Abbey are carved next to the arms of France, as a reminder of the community's loyalty to the monarchy.

The only thoroughfare on the island, the **Grande Rue** or High Street, curves up to the abbey between old houses. The souvenir trade was already flourishing at the time of the great pilgrimages ; shops were filled with scallop shells and holy pictures. Not far from the **house of Tiphaine Raguenel,** wife of the warrior Du Guesclin, stands the **parish church,** which has undergone alteration on several occasions in its history. It contains 15th century statues of Saint Anne and of the Virgin Mary.

The **Great Outer Staircase** (Grand Degré Extérieur) leads to the monastery where the **outer bailey** is flanked by two towers. Building work on this particular part of the abbey was finished in 1393 but the entire project took five centuries to complete (11th-16th). The Romanesque building is perched on the top of the rock above the remains of the Carolingian church. The Romanesque monastic buildings were constructed on the north side and, for many years, the abbey entrance faced north-west. In the Gothic era, new accommodation for the monks was added : this was the "Marvel". The Abbot's apartments were on the opposite side of the monastery, facing south and south-west. And so a real labyrinth came into being, a labyrinth composed of several storeys dating from as many centuries.

The **Abyss Staircase** (Escalier du Gouffre) leads to the 13th century **Guardroom** (Salle des Gardes) with its vaulted ceiling and huge 15th century fireplace. Pilgrims used to leave their weapons here. On the floor above, the Abbots established the **Hall of the Magnificent Throne** (Salle de Belle-Chaise) so-called because of the seat from which they used to dispense justice.

Two bridges connecting the Abbey's administration block to the church span the **Great Inner Staircase** (Grand Degré Intérieur) as it wends its way up the rock to **Gautier's Leap** (Saut Gautier), a platform from which a prisoner jumped to his death.

The 11th century **abbey church** lost three spans from its nave in the 18th century. The Maurists built a new façade in the Classical style, opening onto the platform known as the **'Plomb du Four'** (recent work has uncovered the base of two Romanesque towers which once flanked the façade, as in Jumièges Abbey). The bell-tower, which was struck by lightning, was

Tocqueville : *the castle.*

replaced in the 19th century by an ornate steeple bearing a statue of Saint Michael by Frémiet.

Inside the church, there are markedly contrasting styles. The Romanesque nave is austere, its decoration subdued, and the wood of its barrel-vaulting blends in with the coloured granite used for the columns and galleries. As for the Flamboyant Gothic chancel and radiating chapels, they are a supreme example of lightness and elegance. A finely-sculpted triforium* runs round the chancel above the slender arches.

On the intermediate storey, the **Monks' Ambulatory** with its pointed arches supported by a double row of columns, was originally the cloisters. The **dormitory** was in what is now the sacristy. On the lower storey, the **Northern Crypt** (Crypte de l'Aquilon), where the mighty columns are very simply decorated, was the pilgrims' almonry in the 12th century when the abbey entrance faced north-west.

The church stands above several crypts, all of which are of an earlier period. To the west are the remains of the pre-Romanesque church of **Our-Lady-Underground** (Notre-Dame-sous-Terre) which has two naves. On the south side, the 12th century **Saint Stephen's Chapel** (chapelle Saint-Etienne) served as an ossuary and was situated near the dungeons built by Robert de Torigni. In the 19th century, the enormous wooden wheel housed in the former chapel was used as a winch. The 11th century barrel-vaulted Saint Martin's Crypt beneath the south crossing was used as a reservoir. Beneath the north crossing is the **Crypt of Our Lady of the Thirty Candles** (Notre-Dame-des-Trente-Cierges). Under the chancel, constructed on what was probably the site of an old Romanesque crypt, is the **Crypt of the Mighty Pillars** (Crypte des Gros Piliers) which supports the upthrust of the Gothic building on enormous

116

Saint-Martin-de-Boscherville : *the lantern-tower of the church of Saint-Georges-de-Boscherville.*

stone shafts some 15ft. in circumference.

The chevet, completed c. 1521, is decorated with luxurious foliage, and it seems that architect and sculptor worked in complete harmony. The aptly-named **Lace Stairway** (escalier de dentelles) wends its way between pinnacles* and traceried piers.

Built on the north-facing wall of rock between 1211 and 1228, the "Marvel", a remarkable example of Gothic religious architecture, enclosed all the existing buildings. Like the original monastery, it has three storeys.

At the top, Raoul de Villedieu's **cloisters** gave the monks an opportunity for meditation in a grandiose setting. Two staggered rows of colonettes elegantly support the arches and their corner-stones* which are finely decorated with sculpted foliage or human faces. The cloisters were to lead into the chapter house but it was never built. Thanks to Raoul des Iles, the barrel-vaulting of the ceiling in the **refectory** is supported by thick walls into which were cut slender windows flooding the large hall with light without diminishing its overall strength. During meals, which were taken in silence, one of the monks would read sacred texts from the pulpit.

Immediately underneath the refectory, the **Guests' Hall** (Salle des Hôtes) in which the Abbot welcomed his rich visitors, resembles an elegant reception room with recesses in the walls. The Hall is divided in two by slender pillars. A vast fireplace with two hearths was used to cooks the monks' meals and to keep the pilgrims' food warm. The **Knights' Hall** (Salle des Chevaliers) is so-named because of the order of chivalry founded by Louis XI. It was, in fact, the warming-room and scriptorium, the monks' place of work. The four naves are supported on columns with finely-sculpted capitals.

A spiral staircase leads down to the **cellar** on the lower storey, where the provisions were kept. Under the Guests' Hall is the **hospitium,** or almonry, built by Abbot Jourdain. The large hall with its two naves and groined vaulting dates back to the early 13th century, and it was originally used to provide temporary accommodation for poor pilgrims. Now it houses an exhibition of models retracing the various stages in the history of the building of the Abbey.

Overlooking the Great Outer Staircase is the **Claudine Tower** which leads to the ramparts, built between the 13th and 15th centuries to ensure the impregnability of the Mont Saint-Michel. From the **Gire Terrace,** the visitor reaches the walkway round the walls. There are marvellous views across the bay and over the south face of the Mont. On the north side of the rock, there is a copse and, beyond it, **Saint Aubert's Spring.** To the west, is **Saint Aubert's Chapel,** built on a rock high above the shore.

A walk alone across the sands is not to be recommended. The tale is still told of a reckless young woman who was expecting a child and who was so frightened by the rising tide that she went into labour. Luckily Saint Michael came to her aid and the waves spared the woman. She named her child Peril.

The tiny offshore island of **Tombelaine** had its own priory in the 12th century, later transformed into a castle for Louis XIV's intendant, Fouquet, before being pulled down. Its name may be connected with an old love story. When Hélène de Terregate learned that her lover, the knight Montgomery, had been killed in battle, she fell down dead on the shore and was buried on the same spot, henceforth known as "Tomba Helena".

MONTIVILLIERS (Seine-Maritime)
6 miles N.E. of Le Havre

This small industrial town near Le Havre, built on both banks of the R. Lézarde, originally grew up around a 7th century abbey founded by Saint Philibert. This explains how it got its name, the "monastery town".

The old convent buildings have disappeared among the houses ; only **Saint Saviour's Church** (église Saint-Sauveur) still remains. It was built in the 11th century and extended in the 16th. The façade has kept one of the Romanesque bell-towers and a Romanesque doorway. There is also a Flamboyant porch dating from the late-15th century. A mighty Romanesque lantern-tower was built over the crossing. The Romanesque nave was reserved for the nuns, as was the transept and chancel. After being given over to the parishioners in 1241, the church was found to be too small and a Gothic side-aisle was added. The end wall supports a Flamboyant gallery.

MORTAIN (Manche)
16 miles S. of Vire.

Formerly a fortress belonging to Count Robert, brother of William the Conqueror, the town of Mortain clings onto an outcrop of rock that juts out above the Cance Gorge, on the borders of the Norman Alps. It was very badly damaged in 1944 when the German forces attacked from the position they had taken up between Falaise and Mortain. This pocket of resistance was cleared up after fierce fighting.

Founded early in the 12th century and rapidly affiliated to the Order of Citeaux, the **White Abbey** (Abbaye Blanche), which is dedicated to the Holy Trinity, followed the reforms introduced by Saint Vital who refused to accept the comfortable living conditions of the black-habited Benedictines ; thus, the nuns took the white habit which was to give the abbeys its name. The Fathers of the Holy Spirit who now live there, have set up a museum of missionary work.

The flat chevet and the chapels opening onto the crossings in the late-12th century **church** are typical of the pure Cistercian architectural layout, which is also evident in the later **chapter-house.** Two sides of the Romanesque **cloisters** with their austere granite colonettes have been saved from destruction, as have the sisters' **refectory** and an 11th century cellar, both of which have groined vaulted ceilings.

Saint Evroult's collegiate church was spared by the air raids. Rebuilt in the 13th century, this church is unusual because it has no transept. The upsweep of the gable end of the façade is reinforced by the lines of the bell-towers. The church's treasure includes a very rare 7th century piece called "Le Chrismale", an Anglo-Irish eucharistial bearing Runic inscriptions.

At several points along the course of the R. Cance, there are picturesque **waterfalls.** From the Little Chapel (Petite Chapelle), there is a panoramic view extending to the Mont Saint-Michel on a very clear day.

The **R. Sée** rises not far from Mortain and its upper reaches wend their way through a gently-undulating landscape.

NEUBOURG (Eure)
12 miles N.W. of Evreux.

The fertile plains of the Neubourg Plateau, which is an extension of the Roumois Plateau, are particularly well-suited to the growing of cereal crops.

Not far from **Neubourg** itself, the village where the politician Dupont de l'Eure was born,is **Battlefield Castle** (château du Champ de Bataille) built on the site of a memorable combat in 936 that opposed Rioulf, Count of the Cotenti, to William Longsword. The imposing 17th century square edifice was built in the Louis XIV style by Alexandre de Créqui. Two identical élongated buildings give an impression of symmetry and balance. They are connected by a gallery wich a porch decorated with sculptures on the side facing the entrance ; on the other side, facing the gardens, there is a grille. The foreparts jut out slightly in the middle of the brick and stone façades built in the Classical style and allying harmony of architectural line with moderation of embellishment. The vast rooms house antique furniture and paintings by the old masters.

The grounds of **Harcourt** Castle were given to an ancestor of the illustrious family in the 10th century by Rollo. The 14th century keep, an example of flint bonding, and its two towers, were replaced in the 17th century by a brick façade opening onto a terrace. Several towers and postern gates* in the mediaeval fortifications still exist, as does the parade ground which is enclosed by curtain walls*. In 1828, the castle and wooded parkland became the property of the Academy of Agriculture and an **arboretum** was set up. Several hectares of park were planted with foreign species, particularly conifers.

Saint-Germain-de-Livet : *the entrance to the castle.*

NEUFCHATEL-EN-BRAY (Seine-Maritime)
22 miles S.E. of Dieppe.

Situated on a bank of the R. Béthune, the former capital of the Bray Region, now an agricultural town rebuilt after the Second World War, is a centre of the dairy industry specialising in the production of cottage cheese. Its constant high quality is ensured by the rich pastureland nearby. The castle which gave the town its name was destroyed in the late-16th century.

Building work on the Renaissance castle of **Mesnières-en-Bray,** now an Agricultural College, was started at the end of the 15th century by Louis de Boissay, a relative of the Cardinal d'Amboise. It was then four-sided but, in the 18th century, one of the sides was replaced by a grand staircase. The architectural severity of the towers, which is reminiscent of the chateau of Chaumont-sur-Loire, is in stark contrast to the almost Classical façade overlooking the courtyard. The animal sculptures in the **Deer Gallery** all have real antlers.

NORMAN ALPS

One of the most characteristic regions in the province, the Bocage, has been nicknamed the Norman Alps (somewhat exaggeratedly) because of its hilly terrain, vegetation, pastures and forests. This is a popular tourist area astride the county boundaires of Calvados and Orne, with its own particular brand of charm thanks to the many rivers which run through it, especially the R. Orne. Its meanders are enclosed in a winding valley at the foot of rocky scarp slopes.

Le Val-Richer : *the façade of the restored part of the former abbey.*

From **Putanges-Pont-Ecrepin,** a village specialising in leatherwork, to Thury-Harcourt, the river has hollowed out gullies in the old rocks, such as **Saint Aubert's Gorge.**

High above the confluence of the rivers Rouvre and Orne, the wild setting of **Oëtre Rock** is equally impressive. Further downstream lies **Clécy,** the main centre for touring the area. The **Faverie Cross** (Croix de la Faverie) and **Sugar Loaf** (Pain de Sucre) overlook the river. Nearby, **Placy Manor** (16th century) now houses the Normandy Museum.

NORMANDY LANDING BEACHES — see CALVADOS (COAST OF)

O (Orne)
approx. 6 miles S.E. of Argentan.

Situated **not far from Mortrée,** the elegant Castle of O is reflected in the wide moat which surrounds it. The building was begun in the 15th century but underwent alteration on several occasions until the 18th century. The mansion was the home of François d'O, Superintendant of Finance and favourite of Henri III, a courtier who scandalised others at court by the life of luxury and ostentation he led at the State's expense.

The gateway through the oldest wing of the building stands in the midst of lodges and turrets. The roof is particularly high and the walls are an example of checkerboard bonding in stone and brick. One of the attic windows displays elements from the Flamboyant, or late Gothic, period alongside early examples of Italian-inspired ornamentation. A finely-

121

decorated Renaissance gallery opening onto the courtyard leads to the main building which dates from 1770.

OUISTREHAM — RIVA-BELLA (Calvados)
9 miles N.E. of Caen.

The yachting marina of this international sailing centre and fishing port on the estuary of the R. Orne and the Caen Canal, forms part of a bustling seaside resort which also includes the long sandy beach of Riva-Bella.

The once-battlemented **church,** which underwent restoration after the Liberation of France, combines two architectural styles : its façade and nave (it has no transept) are Romanesque, while its chancel is in an early-Gothic style characteristic of the Norman School.

It was on the beach at **Riva-Bella** ("Sword Beach") where the sea goes two miles out at low tide, that the troops led by the British commander, Kieffer, landed on 6th June 1944 before joining up with the parachutists who had gained control of the bridge of Bénouville ("Pegasus Bridge").

Bénouville **Castle,** a large Neo-classical edifice designed by Nicolas Ledoux (18th century), is an imposing building four storeys high. Overlooking the courtyard is a peristyle* with Ionic columns.

PERCHE

The Perche (capital : Nogent-le-Rotrou) is a transitional belt between the Paris Basin and Armorican Moutains, an area of ever-changing rolling scenery, where the climate and natural irrigation have encouraged the growth of dense vegetation. This is the cradle of emigration to Canada ; one of the earliest settlers was the Norman, Pierre Boucher.

In the wooded valleys of the Upper, or **Norman, Perche** are rich grazing lands dotted with manor-houses. The Lower Perche, also called the **Perche-Gouët** after a mediaeval lord of the manor, slopes down to the Beauce Plain.

The home town of Alain, the philosopher, **Mortagne-au-Perche,** was once one of the main towns in the county, along with Bellême and Nogent-le-Rotrou. Built on a site high above the valley of the R. Huisne, which was occupied by a monastery as far back as the 7th century, the town is a centre of horse-trading and riding. It is also famous for its black pudding, a gastronomic delight when served with a cream sauce ('à la normande') or grilled and served with apples. **Notre Dame Church** is a combination of Renaissance and Flamboyant architecture. The stalls and panelling in the chancel come from the Carthusian monastery of Val-Dieu.

Longny-au-Perche nestles deep in the valley of the R. Jambée, not far from the forest. A large stairway leads to the **Chapel of Mercy** (Chapelle de la Pitié) which has a finely-decorated Renaissance porch.

The former mediaeval walled city of Bellême, now an important market-town, stands on a spur of rock overlooking the forest. Its houses face onto the R. Même, a tributary of the Huisne. For many years, it had very close ties with the Dukes of Normandy and the House of the wealthy Lords of Bellême was influential throughout the region for several centuries.

In 1229, Blanche of Castille and her son Louis IX attacked the fortress. It was rebuilt in the 15th century but only the gateway into the town still remains. Seventeenth — and eighteenth — century town houses, often displaying some ornamentation, stand on the site of the former citadel. Aristide Boucicaut, father of one of the large Parisian department stores, the "Bon Marché", was born in Bellême.

The regional forests are mainly oak and beech ; some of the trees are almost three hundred years old (as in the **Réno-Valdieu** forest near Mortagne). The **Bellême Forest,** which the author Roger Martin-du-Gard (who died in Bellême) once described as "mysterious and alive" has a large number of footpaths.

PIN (STUD)

It was in 1669 that Colbert founded the Pin Stud, now a famous centre of horse-breeding. In 1861, a thoroughbred called Gladiator brought it a moment of glory by winning the Epsom Derby.

The 'Versailles of the Horse World', which so delighted the writer La Varende, was built between 1715 and 1728 on a 2,470-acre site to the north of the Ure Valley. The plans were drawn up by Mansart and the buildings overlook the terraces and paths laid out by Le Nôtre. Magnificent bridlepaths converge on the horseshoe-shaped main courtyard.

Every year, a horse show is held here, and the races which are run at the beginning of October are always followed by the traditional horse-and-rider procession in which six different breeds of stallion take part.

PONT-L'EVEQUE (Calvados)
7 miles S.E. of Trouville-Deauville.

In the heart of the Auge Region at the confluence of the rivers Touques, Calonne and Yvie, lies Pont-l'Evêque, once an important road junction. Bishop Hugh of Lisieux had the first bridge built over the R. Touques in 1070, hence the name of the town (Bishop's Bridge).

Its strong-smelling cheese was famous as far back as the 13th century when it was known as "angelot". In the 19th century, the Pont-l'Evêque Fairs delighted the author Stendhal. Flaubert often came here to stay with relations on his mother's side. It was also the birthplace of the comedy-writer Robert de Flers. He was born in the Brilly Town-house (now the Town Hall). A **Museum of Saddlery** is a reminder of the importance of horse-breeding in this region.

Founded in the 11th century by Hugh de Montfort, **Saint Hymer's Priory** was one of the daughter-houses of the Bec Abbey. It increased its sphere of influence in the 18th century when it became known as the "Port-Royal of Normandy", a centre of Jansenist thinking developed by Abbot de Roquette. The prior restored the monastic buildings, the cloisters, and the 14th century church, and founded a library.

In **Saint-André-d'Hébertot,** the 17th century keep of Auguessau Castle stands in the middle of extensive grounds.

The **Touques Valley** which runs from Pont-l'Evêque to the coast, crosses orchards and grazing land dotted with manor-houses and timber-framed houses.

RISLE (VALLEY)

After crossing the wooded plateau of the Ouche Region, with its outcrops of hard limestone*, the R. Risle runs uphill and down dale through a whole string of villages, small towns and urban communities like Brionne and Pont-Audemer, until it reaches the Seine Estuary.

Legend has it that a bell, which has been on the riverbed since the Hundred Years' War, still rings as if to echo the chimes of **Corneville,** which are based on those of the famous operetta by R. Planquette.

The Benedictine Priory of the Holy Trinity in **Beaumont-le-Roger** was founded by one of William the Conqueror's counsellors, Roger de Beaumont, who gave his name to the town. Perched on a terrace supported by mighty piers, the priory is reached by a steep ramp. One wall and the impressive gable end of the chevet are all that remain of the church.

Rouen : *faïence from the Levavasseur pottery (late 18th century).*

◀ **Rouen :** *the Great Clock.*

ROUEN (Seine-Maritime)
88 miles N.W. of Paris and 53 miles E. of Le Havre.

Rouen is a multifaceted town : open-air museum, capital of Upper Normandy and county town of Seine-Maritime, fourth-largest port in France, a city midway between Paris and the coast at the very heart of a large communications network. It has managed to preserve its rich and prestigious history while looking resolutely to the future. Although the city of a hundred bells attracts a large number of tourists to the old town on the right bank of the R. Seine, it was given a totally new look last century when major roads were built and industrialisation arrived. Post-war reconstruction and the economic expansion of the region as a whole have both promoted the development of a whole new town on the left bank of the river and, with it, the expansion of Rouen into a large urban and suburban community with more than five hundred thousand inhabitants.

Its location between the Cailly and Robec valleys on a meander of the Seine, where small islands facilitated river-crossings, had already been chosen by the Veliocasses as a particularly suitable site for their settlement. Ratumacos ('the place of exchange'), renamed Rotomagus under the Romans, had its first bishop, Mellon, in 260 A.D. and became the administrative centre of a vast area. Merovingian monarchs stayed in the town during hunting parties in the neighbouring forests. The town was also at the heart of a region much influenced by monasticism, and the movement was given additional impetus by two bishops, Saint Romain (patron

125

saint of the town) and Saint Ouen. Thus the town enjoyed a period of prosperity and development that was to last until the Viking invasions.

After the signing of the Treaty of Saint-Clair-sur-Epte in 911 by which the King of France ceded Normandy to Rollo, the Viking chief, the new head of the region decided to set up residence in Rouen, which thereby became the political, administrative and religious capital of the duchy and an important business centre. It was to retain these rôles for more than a thousand years.

The prosperity that the Dukes of Normandy and Kings of England brought to the town came to an end as a result of the One Hundred Years' War. In 1418, after a long cruel siege during which the English army starved the inhabitants into submission, the town was forced to surrender. Another dramatic episode was the trial of Joan of Arc, who organised resistance to the invaders and led troops loyal to the King of France. She was burnt at the stake in Old Market Square on 30th May 1431. The King, Charles VII, did not retake Rouen until 1449.

Then came a new era, called the "Golden Age", the result not only of maritime and mercantile trade but also of the influence exerted by Cardinal Georges I of Amboise, one of Louis XII's ministers, who was to introduce the Italian Renaissance into Rouen. This period of tranquillity was broken by the Wars of Religion which heralded more troubled times (especially as the town had a large Protestant community).

The Fronde revolt, epidemics, and the Revocation of the Edict of Nantes in 1685 which forced many craftsmen and traders into exile, all had a disastrous effect on the town's economy. It was to remain depressed until the 18th century which saw the start of the textile industry ('rouenneries' or printed cottons replaced chintzes), and the introduction of ceramic-ware with motifs based on embroidery (the Edicts had obliged citizens to melt down their silverware and they had replaced it with faïence). In the 19th century, the harbour was developed (it has recently been modernised).

The town did not escape the last war unscathed : the old town was very badly damaged but has since been carefully and skilfully restored. Contemporary buildings compete in size and architectural design with grand historical edifices, in a blend of old and new.

Rouen is, above all, a sea- and river-port supplying Paris, as seems only natural. Its exceptional situation as the French capital's lower harbour has been reinforced by a large number of facilities (warehouses, refineries, factories and floating docks) which are strung out along the wharves ready to receive large bulk carriers and to handle commodities such as wood, oil, cereals, citrus fruit, wine and ore. Iron foundries, petrochemical plants, and textile factories have been built on the river banks, and, to this list of industries must be added cotton (the oldest of Rouen's manufacturing enterprises), a large output of newsprint, and shipyards.

Gourmets will be interested in the local specialities : apple-flavoured barley sugar, desserts such as "douillons" and "rabottes" (pear and apple dumplings), and main courses such as "canard en sang" (jugged duckling) served with a cream and apple-brandy sauce.

The town was a regional centre of intense literary and artistic activity very early in its history, and was the birthplace of many celebrities. Among them are the 17th century poet M.-A. de Saint-Amant, the actress Champmeslé, a number of writers including Pierre and Thomas Corneille, N. Pradon (Racine's great rival) ; Fontenelle, Villemessant, Flaubert (whose father was surgeon-in-chief at the local hospital), M. Leblanc (who created the character Arsène Lupin), and A. Salacrou. Other famous sons of Rouen are the painters J. Restout and Géricault, the architect Blondel, and the musicians Boïeldieu and M. Dupré.

The **Cathedral of Our Lady** (Notre Dame), a complex building of imposing dimensions displaying the whole gamut of Gothic design, gives an overall impression of order despite mutilation and the variations in style (the façade was immortalised in the famous series of paintings by Claude Monet). The cathedral was restored after the bombing raids in 1944 and is now part of our national heritage by virtue of its outstanding architectural value and the richness of its decoration.

The earliest cathedral was built by Saint Vitricius at the end of the 4th century. A Romanesque building, of which only the crypt under the chancel remains, replaced the original church and was consecrated in 1063 in the presence of Duke William. The 12th century saw the beginning of yet another cathedral : Saint Romain's Tower was built in 1145, followed by the façade (c. 1170), the nave (1185 onwards) and finally the chancel and transept, which were damaged by fire in 1200 and not completed until 1247. In the 14th and 15th centuries, the cathedral underwent alteration and enlargement (Butter Tower). The central doorway and the tombs in the Lady Chapel were completed in the 16th century.

The main façade is an early example of Flamboyant architecture, superimposed on the basic structure in which the English influence is manifest. It is bristling with bell-turrets and flanked by two very different towers : **Saint Romain's Tower,** which has an Early Gothic base (12th century), and the exuberantly Flamboyant **Butter Tower** (tour de Beurre) which was begun in the late-15th century by Guillaume Pontifs and finished in the 16th century. It was paid for by money from dispensations granted to the faithful who wanted to eat butter during Lent. The Butter Tower has a 56-bell peal. Between the two 12th century sculpted side porches is the main doorway built by Roulland Le Roux in the 16th century. It is decorated with a Tree of Jesse and a large number of statuettes, and is surmounted by a tall pierced gable* above which is the central rose window.

The portals of the transept were built between 1280 and 1340 and have conserved their sculpted tympanums, statuettes and whimsical bas-reliefs. The **Calende Portal** to the south, flanked by towers, counterbalances the **Booksellers' Portal** (portail des Libraires) in the north transept, so-called because of the numerous bookstalls in the adjoining courtyard. The decoration of the doorway is surprisingly spirited. Above the crossing, the 13th century lanter-tower, which has since undergone alteration, rises to more than 490 ft. (it has a height of 165 ft. up to the vaulting).

The mighty Early Gothic **nave,** four storeys high, is incomplete for its galleries were never built. The side-aisles lead into a transept with very ornate gable-ends. To the north is the Bookshop Staircase (escalier de la Librairie), the work of Guillaume Pontifs. The 13th century **chancel,** which lies above the now-open Romanesque crypt, allies simplicity of style and purity of line. The stained glass in the ambulatory also dates from the 13th century (the window depicting Saint John the Hospitaler provided the theme of one of Flaubert's novels). In the Lady Chapel are the famous **tombs of the Cardinals of Amboise** (Georges I and II), which are masterpieces of early Renaissance sculpture (beginning of the 16th century) and which are based on the work of Roulland le Roux. In the same chapel is the later tomb of **Louis de Brézé,** husband of Diane de Poitiers. A painting by Philippe de Champaigne hangs on the wall.

Saint Maclou's (or Malo's) **Church** is a homogeneous building in the Flamboyant Gothic style although it dates, in fact, from the Renaissance 15th and 16th centuries. It was constructed according to plans drawn up by Pierre Robin. The Duke of Bedford was instrumental in its construction. Its porch, with a pierced gable*, precedes three entrances, two of which have very ornate Renaissance doors*. Inside the church, a finely-carved Flamboyant spiral staircase, taken originally from a rood-screen, leads to an organ loft decorated with Renaissance panelling.

Near the church is a rare and very fine example of a mediaeval ossuary, the **Aître Saint-Maclou,** which was built in the 16th century after an epidemic. It resembles cloisters, comprising as it does timbered galleries originally open on one side, and pillars decorated with sculptures of a Danse Macabre and funereal ornamentation. The skeletons were taken to the upper storey, once a loft. Nowadays, the building houses an Art College.

Saint Ouen's Church, a 14th century minster, is one of the treasures of French Gothic architecture. The memory of Saint Ouen, a former army officer who became a bishop and

Troarn : *the abbey.*

undisputed head of the Norman church in the 7th century, ensured that the monastery's influence was long-lasting. It was in 916 that Duke Rollo had the saint's relics brought to Rouen from Condé and that, as a token of submission and humility, he walked barefoot at the head of the procession. It was mysteriously held up some miles out of town by a divine force. Later, Rollo donated all the land that he had crossed to pay for services of worship.

Several buildings were erected on the same site. The 11th century edifice, given to the Benedictine Order by an abbot who was a cousin of William the Conqueror, was burnt down. All that remains today is a Romanesque apsidal chapel and the Clerks' Tower.

The present church, which is bigger than the cathedral, was begun in 1318 under Abbot Marc d'Argent, and finished in the 15th century. Apart from the main façade, which was built in the 19th century, the architectural style is fairly uniform. The lightness of the chevet with its pinnacles* and arches, is reflected in the elegant two-storey central tower or **'crowned tower'** which is surmounted by a ducal coronet. In the south crossing of the almost flat transept is the **Urchins' Portal** (porche des Marmousets) ; here, the vaulting springs from pendants, and small bas-reliefs retell story of Saint Ouen's life. Legend has it that murder was committed on account of the rose windows, for the apprentice is said to have produced better work than his teacher, a jealous master glass-painter. It is, however, more likely that they are the work of Berneval Sr. and his son.

The interior is striking for its overall harmony, the efforts to ensure the suffusion of light, and the slenderness of the arches. The radiating chancel (14th century) was given an open-work triforium* which was an innovation in its day. At one end of the 16th century nave are the Cavallé-Coll organs. The **town hall** offices now occupy the 18th century monastic buildings.

Among the town's lay monuments, the **Law Courts** are undoubtedly the most outstanding by virtue of their exuberant ornamentation. It can be seen as a stepping-stone between the Gothic and Renaissance styles (it suffered extensive damage in 1940). The Courts were built in the early 16th century, probably by Roulland le Roux, to house the Exchequer of Normandy, which was reorganised under Louis XII when it became a permanent court of justice. The assembly, which has been responsible for running the financial and administrative affairs of the Duchy since the 12th century, was originally a feudal court. The name 'exchequer' was derived from a checkered cloth used when the court was in session and on which the accounts were tallied with counters. The assembly kept the title until it became a Parliament under François I. In England, where the Kings were also Dukes of Normandy, the title "Chancellor of the Exchequer" is still given to the Finance Minister.

The decoration of the **façade** overlooking the main courtyard becomes increasingly ornate towards the upper stories until, at roof level, it verges on the unimaginable. The Neo-Gothic wings are 19th century. Restoration work in the **Attorney's Hall** (Salle des Procureurs) has given it back its original Gothic nave-like appearance. An early-12th century Hebrew monument has been uncovered beneath the courtyard.

The same 'lacework' style is in evidence at the 16th century **Bourgtheroulde House.** It has a Renaissance gallery on which carvings retell the tale of the Meeting of the Field of the Cloth of Gold.

In the heart of the town's shopping centre is **Old Market Square** (Place du Vieux-Marché) whose name has become synonymous with Joan of Arc, patron saint of France. The square has recently been redeveloped, so that now the church and memorial to the saint add a contemporary note to the memories which have accumulated here over the centuries.

After imprisonment in the keep of the feudal castle built in the reign of Philippe Auguste (Joan of Arc's Tower is still standing), where she was guarded by English gaolers, and after repeated questioning, the Maid of Orleans was proclaimed by Bishop Cauchon to be a witch and a heretic ; she was condemned to death. The site of the stake is marked by a tall cross.

Saint Joan of Arc's Church, designed by Louis Arretche, is a blend of ancient and modern ; Renaissance glass has been incorporated into a daringly stark building. The fanciful picturesque series of windows (especially those by Enguerrand le Prince which are particularly graphic) was brought from the chancel of Saint Vincent's Church after it was destroyed in 1944.

Pedestrian precincts lead from Old Market Square to Saint Maclou's Church. **Old timbered houses,** most of which have recently been restored, are a feature of the surrounding streets, like Saint Romain's, la Ganterie (Glovers') and Gros-Horloge (Great Clock). The last of the three has been the busiest thoroughfare in the town since Roman times.

Amid the hustle and bustle, the **Great Clock** (Gros-Horloge) and adjoining Gothic belfry draw the attention of all the passers-by. The elegant Renaissance construction spanning the roadway is decorated on both sides by a gilded lead dial with a single hand. In a niche, there is a bas-relief which changes every twenty-four hours and which depicts the god of each day of the week.

There are many other monuments worthy of the visitor's attention, e.g. the **Fierte Saint-Romain,** a 16th century Renaissance building in the Greco-Roman style designed to house the relics of the former bishop. In days gone by, it was customary to grant a pardon to one condemned man after the sacred reliquary had been carried in procession round the town.

However, Rouen also has some remarkable museums which should not go unnoticed.

In the **Fine Arts Museum** (musée des Beaux-Arts), a comprehensive collection of faïence enables the visitor to follow the expansion of the craft from its earliest days and to see the various styles developed by local potteries. The museum also contains examples of all the major schools of painting, especially from the 19th century (the Géricault Room, the J.-E. Blanche Room). Local artists hang alongside the great Impressionist painters (Monet, Pissaro, Sisley, Lebourg).

The **Le Secq des Tourelles Museum,** which is housed in what was formerly Saint Lawrence's Church, has an outstanding collection of wrought-iron work.

In the **Seine-Maritime Museum of Antiquity,** gold plate, ivory, sculpted reliefs and tapestry are displayed near the great mosaic of Lillebonne and the Gallo-Roman exhibition.

In the immediate vicinity of Rouen, the large number of vantage points along the cliff road all give the tourist an equally breathtaking, but quite different, view of the town. We shall mention only two : **Bonsecours** and **Saint Catherine's Hill** (côte Sainte-Catherine), from which one looks straight down over the city and a meander of the R. Seine.

Near **Canteleu,** which Maupassant found particularly attractive, a small Louis XV pavilion is all that remains of Flaubert's estate in **Croisset.** It contains memorabilia of the author. In **Petit-Couronne,** Corneille's country residence is open to the public ; it is a 17th century timbered manor-house.

Situated to the North of Rouen, near a Motor Museum, the **Clères** wild life park is famous for its large collection of tropical birds.

SAINT-GEORGES-DE-BOSCHERVILLE (Seine-Maritime)
6 miles from the Left Bank of Rouen.

Near the Roumare Forest, the place of worship in the village of **Saint-Martin-de-Boscherville** is, in fact, the **church** of the former abbey of **Saint-Georges-de-Boscherville** which was founded in 1050 by Raoul de Tancarville, chamberlain to William the Conqueror. In 1114, Benedictines from Saint Evroult replaced the regular canons.

The building, which was completed in 1125, possesses an overall uniformity of style which makes it an outstanding example of purely Norman Romanesque architecture. The only alterations are in the nave and transept where the original beams were replaced by ogival arches in the 13th century. The main entrance, which is very plain with geometric designs decorating the arching*, is in stark contrast to the mighty lantern-tower above the transept crossing. Inside the church, decoration is restricted to friezes outlining the arches and two antique bas-reliefs beneath the galleries in the transept.

The 12th century **chapter-house** and the 17th century building above it look onto a well which once marked the centre of cloisters. The finely-sculpted arches of the three Renaissance bays rest on colonettes with elaborately-decorated capitals. The badly-mutilated column statues, which are the only ones of their kind in Normandy, are reminiscent of those in Chartres.

SAINT-GERMAIN-DE-LIVET (Calvados)
5 miles S. of Lisieux.

In the Touques Valley to the south of Lisieux stands Saint-Germain-de-Livet Castle, surrounded by a moat, one of the most characteristic examples of Auge regional architecture still in existence. The late-16th century building is a chequerboard of white stone, and green, pink or yellow brick and glazed tiles from the Pré d'Auge.

In the timbered wing, which is a century older than the rest of the castle, the Guard Room is decorated with sculptures and there are traces of 16th century friezes. On the first floor, there is an example of typical Pré d'Auge tiling, and memorabilia of the painter Delacroix.

SAINT-LO (Manche)
36 miles W. of Caen.

The county town of Manche perched on an outcrop of shale overlooking the Vire river valley was named Briovère ('bridge over the Vire') by the Gauls ; its founders established a settlement on the site because of its strategic position. In the 6th century, the town took the name of the bishop of Coutances, Saint-Lô, for it was by then in possession of his relics and was therefore a place of pilgrimage. In 1574, during the Wars of Religion, Saint-Lô underwent a memorable siege led by Marshall de Matignon.

Its situation at the centre of a road and rail network meant that it was at the hub of German resistance to Allied troops in June 1944. While 'hedge warfare' was being waged in the wooded countryside round about, the town was shelled by the American forces until it fell on July 19th. The Battle of Saint-Lô had transformed it into a pathetic 'capital of ruins'.

However, the new town soon emerged, including the Enclosure, or 'Enclos', an area surrounded by fortifications which had been uncovered by the bombing. Visitors can now stroll along the ramparts.

The twin towers of **Notre Dame Church** have purposefully been left in their 1944 condition to serve as a reminder of the powerful explosions caused by the shelling. The remainder of the building (13th-17th century) has been restored. A Flamboyant pulpit on the outside of the church was used for the publication of episcopal decrees.

The **Museum** houses a complete collection of tapestries illustrating « The Love Affair of Gombart and Macée » (16th century).

English and French stallions are selected at the National **Stud,** and an International Horse Show takes place in May every year.

SAINT-PIERRE-SUR-DIVES (Calvados)
18 miles S.W. of Lisieux.

This large rural community, which used to be called L'Epinay (in olden days, thorns (épines) were often found growing at crossroads), lies in a transitional agricultural and dairy-farming area between the Caen and Auge Regions. The priest of Saint Peter's Church, later to be canonised under the name of Saint Wambert, was martyred by the Vikings in the 9th century. The town took the name of the parish and thereafter its history was closely intertwined with that of its Benedictine abbey. It has kept up the traditional tanning trade to this day, and most of the packaging for Normandy's cheese is manufactured here. It is also famous for its old apple-brandy. The Gothic **covered market** was restored after the last war.

It was in the 11th century that Duke Richard II's sister-in-law, Lesceline, founded a **convent** in the castle which her deceased husband had not had time to finish. In 1050, the nuns were replaced by monks of the Benedictine Order, who built the **church** of which one Romanesque tower is still standing. The church was burnt down in the 12th century and was rebuilt. Most of it, including the lantern-tower, is 13th century Gothic but it underwent alteration on several occasions. During the Renaissance, choir stalls and carved misericords* were added to the chancel. An attractive 13th century glazed brick pavement was removed from the chancel and placed in the **chapter-house.**

SAINT-WANDRILLE (Seine-Maritime)
22 miles N.W. of Rouen.

Notre-Dame-de-Fontenelle Abbey, in Saint-Wandrille-Rançon, was founded in 649 by a former dignitary of King Dagobert, called Wandrille. The site chosen is a tranquil spot through which flows the R. Fontanelle.

Ransom money was paid to the Vikings and the abbey was thus saved from looting for many years. However, it was destroyed in 858 and, when it was rebuilt in the 10th century, it took the name of its founder. In the Middle Ages, the abbey was both influential and prosperous, by virtue of the reputation of its teaching and its rich agricultural lands. Saved from ruin in the 17th century by Maurist monks, it was again devastated and transformed during the

French Revolution.

The writer M. Maeterlinck rented it for several years and, in 1909, put on theatrical productions using as their blackcloth the galleries, ruins and park of the monastery. Since 1931, it has been brought back to monasticism by a congregation of Benedictines who have revived the Gregorian chant.

Visitors enter the abbey by the great gateway and the imposing 18th century **Jarente door.**

Of the 13th and 14th century **Gothic church,** only ruins and one arm of the transept now remain. But the Flamboyant-style cloisters still exist ; one of the galleries is 14th century, the others date from the 15th. On the north side, nearest the Romanesque refectory, is a sumptuous **lavabo** decorated with fine sculpture reminiscent of the Renaissance period and Italian taste.

The monks live in the 17th century **monastic buildings** and have established their church in an old tithe barn brought from Neuville-du-Bosc (Eure). A modern reliquary contains the bones of Saint Wandrille.

To reach **Saint Saturnin's Chapel,** the visitor follows a path round the outside of the estate. The chapel is a reminder of the Carolingian era, but it also bears witness to the early days of Romanesque art in Normandy (10th century). The façade was restored in the 16th century. It is a discreet but robust building perched on the hillside. The bonding used was rather unusual as it is in the form of fish-bones. The clover-leaf layout is based on an earlier construction. The decoration is a combination of foliage and sculpted friezes displaying fantastic animals.

SEES (Orne)
13 miles N.E. of Alençon.

Sées, or Séez, situated near the source of the R. Orne in the heart of rich farmland, was once the main settlement of the Sagi people. Since the 4th century, it has been a bishopric and its numerous places of worship have been preserved in an atmosphere of pious devotion.

A typical example of the 13th and 14th century Gothic style is **Notre Dame Cathedral** which stands beside the former bishop's palace. The façade was altered on several occasions and, in front of it, is a deep porch. Enormous piers had to be added to the building in the 16th century to combat subsidence.

Between the great arches in the nave, the corner-stones* are decorated with sculptures of leaves and plants. Above them is a blind storey* like the one in Bayeux and Ardenne. In the transept and chancel, it is pierced. The chancel is bathed in light from the clerestory and from the 13th century stained glass windows and rose windows. The High Altar, which is carved, was made in the reign of Louis XVI.

SEINE (VALLEY OF)

By virtue of its ever-changing landscapes, its rich heritage, its archeological sites and its economic resources, the R. Seine is not only a pivot between Upper and Lower Normandy, but also the centre of gravity of the whole province, for it is the river which links it to the sea and to the capital of France.

The fast-flowing river carries its alluvium through almost 130 miles of meanders between Vernon and Le Havre, where it becomes a wide estuary. Here, the river carved a deep valley into the limestone and its meanders constantly changed course, thus creating a large alluvial plain, overshadowed in many places by steeply-sloping uplands. The inner edge of the bends in the river are mainly covered in woodland ; the many ports are nearly all built on the outer edge of its meanders.

Many settlements sprang up along the valley because of the amount of traffic using the river from the earliest days. Sometimes it formed part of the communications network ;

sometimes it was a frontier. It rôle as a means of transporting goods and passengers, which existed as far back as the Bronze Age, gained in importance from the 6th century onwards with the building of monasteries like Jumièges and Saint-Wandrille on its banks. Later, the Vikings too made use of the waterway to capture the fertile lands through which it flowed, until the King of France finally ceded the Duchy of Normandy to the Viking's Chief, Rollo (911).

Upstream from Rouen, the river crosses the **Norman Vexin,** a region of apple trees broken up by fortresses, churches, castles, and extensive forest. The varied scenery can be fully appreciated from vantage points on the cliff tops (Les Andelys, Two Lovers' Hill).

Beyond Pont-de-l'Arche where the R. Eure flows into the Seine, lies **Elbeuf,** the town in which the writer André Maurois was born. Formerly a centre of the cloth trade, it was rebuilt after the last war (in Saint Stephen's Church there is a 16th century window donated by the drapers). In the 17th century, Colbert set up a Royal Factory in the town, thereby establishing its prosperity. Nowadays, however, it is linked to the adjoining towns, and the conglomeration is dependent on Rouen's industrial estate.

From **Belbeuf,** a small village overlooked by 'dead' cliffs (Saint Adrian's Rocks) in which a chapel was cut in the 13th century, there is a panoramic view of the entire Rouen urban district. It is said that woad, a plant used in the Middle Ages for its colouring properties, is still to be found in the hills.

The 'Abbey Trail' follows the right bank of the river with its wooded hills and cliffs, as the Seine wends its way slowly down to the Channel. Since the 19th century, continual damming work in the alluvium-filled estuary has done away with the tidal bore (cf. Caudebec), so that the very largest ships can now sail upstream to the numerous factory belts, especially in Le Havre and Rouen which form the industrial hub of the **lower reaches of the river.** Economic activity includes textiles, metalworking, electronics and electrical engineering, chemicals, and particularly oil-related industries. Several pipelines run from Le Havre to refineries and to Paris.

The large number of factories does not detract from the scenery and natural beauty spots.

Between the **Orival Rocks,** where falcons still nest and into which cave dwellings have been cut, and the hills of **La Bouille,** stand the ruins of **Robert the Devil's castle,** now a **Viking Museum.** Only two battlemented towers remain of the building dating back to the days of the first Dukes of Normandy. Legend has it that the castle was inhabited by a mythical character who resembled Robert the Magnificent (William the Conqueror's father) but who was, in fact, the son of the Devil.

SILLE-LE-GUILLAUME (Sarthe)
20 miles N.W. of Le Mans.

This the gateway to the Normandy-Maine Regional Park. It lies near a forest on the slopes of the Coëvron Hills, and was once a fortified town. A lake has been equipped for leisure activities.

TANCARVILLE (Seine-Maritime)
18 miles E. of Le Havre.

The feudal castle of Lord Trancrède ("Trancredi Villa") gained importance in the 11th century under Raoul de Tancarville, Chamberlain to William the Conqueror. Standing high on a chalk promontory called the 'Tancarville Nose', it dominated the Seine Estuary. Only the Eagle's Tower now remains from this early fortress. Several 13th and 16th century buidings stand within the outer fortifications, as does an 18th century castle.

Since 1887, the **Tancarville Canal** has enabled barges to reach Le Havre harbour without having to travel along the Estuary.

Thanks to the **suspension bridge** opened in 1959, there is now a direct road from Le Havre to Lower Normandy and Brittany (before the bridge was built, ferries carried traffic across the river), and the region's income from industry and tourism has increased enormously. The bridge is almost a mile long. On the right bank, it rests on the cliff beside the castle. It spans the river to the Vernier Marshes where it is supported by conrete pillars, a real technical feat. The road is 156 ft. above the river.

LE TRÉPORT — EU (Seine-Maritime)
17 miles N.E. of Dieppe.

Situated at the mouth of the R. Bresle on the northernmost border of Normandy, the small fishing port of Le Tréport is a seaside resort which became fashionable when Louis-Philippe built the first villa there. Its beach, adjacent to that of **Mers-les-Bains,** is the nearest beach to Paris. From the top of its chalk cliffs, beside the **Terrace Cross** (Calvaire des Terrasses), there is a panoramic view.

Chosen by William the Conqueror as the setting for his marriage to Matilda in 1050, the old town of **Eu** has grown up on a site between the sea and the forest. In his book, "Pierre Nozière", Anatole France described the charms of this small town near Le Tréport.

The former collegiate **Church of Our Lady and Saint Lawrence** was built in 1181 after the death, in the nearby monastery, of the Primate of Ireland, Lawrence O'Tool. His relics have remained in the church ever since. The church is one of the earliest examples of Gothic architecture in Normandy. The apse was rebuilt in the 15th century and Viollet-le-Duc later undertook general restoration work. The huge crypt houses statues of the Counts of Artois.

The building of the stone and brick Renaissance **castle** was started in 1578 by Henri de Guise on the site of an old fortress in which Joan of Arc is said to have been imprisoned. Enlarged several times, it was the home of the Grande Mademoiselle (the King's niece), and later became a favourite residence of Louis-Philippe who received Queen Victoria there. The King laid out the gardens which had been designed by Le Nôtre, and restored the castle. His grandson, the Count of Paris, had the interior decorated by Viollet-le-Duc. It is now a museum.

In an unusual Louis XIII-style building are the marble mausoleums of the Duke de Guise and his wife ; it is the chapel of the Jesuit College founded by Catherine of Cleves, now the Anguier High School, named after the two famous sculptors who were born in Eu.

A drive through the **Forest of Eu,** where game is abundant, gives the visitor a chance to admire views of the Triage Hills.

VALMONT (Seine-Maritime)
7 miles S.E. oF Fécamp.

The village and river Valmont not far from Fécamp are dominated by the **castle** of the Lords of Estouteville ; a Renaissance wing adjoins the remnants of the mediaeval building.

In 1169, one of their Lordships, Nicolas d'Estouteville, set up the **Abbey** of Valmont on the opposite bank of the river. It was founded for the Benedictine Order. The partly-ruined **church** has a Renaissance chancel which has lost its vaulting and clerestory. But the Lady Chapel, or **Chapel of the Six Hours,** has remained intact and is an absolute gem. Its ornamentation is refined and its vaulting harmonious. Light streams in through Renaissance windows onto the tombs of the founder and Jacques d'Estouteville, and a sculpted Annunciation scene attributed to Germain Pilon.

The painter Delacroix stayed in the Classical-style monastic buildings on several occasions.

134

VALOGNES (Manche)
12 miles S.W. of Cherbourg.

This agricultural and shopping centre in the Cherbourg Peninsula, with its industries based on dairy-farming and timber, grew up on the site of a Gallo-Roman settlement and had its moment of glory in the 17th and 18th centuries when it attracted certain members of the aristocracy, who are savagely criticised in Lesage's book, "Turcaret". Later, Barbey d'Aurevilly too gave a description of Valognes, in his "Chevalier des Touches". Although badly damaged in 1944, the town has preserved some remnants of its glorious past.

The Classical **Beaumont House,** set in formal gardens, was built in the 19th century by Pierre Jallot.

The former Benedictine **Abbey of Our Lady of Protection,** a Louis XIII-style edifice which now houses the hospital, was originally founded in Cherbourg. It was transferred here after the execution of Julien and Marguerite de Ravallet (cf. Tourlaville). The lovers' father and uncle set up the abbey in atonement. The church and cloisters are still in existence.

The **Regional Cider Museum** houses a collection of documents describing the various processes involved in the making of the drink.

A few miles away, the Gothic church of **Colomby** is a simple expression of the Lancet* style of architecture.

VARENGEVILLE (Seine-Maritime)
5 miles E. of Dieppe.

This holiday resort on the Alabaster Coast which actually comprises several tiny villages, has often attracted artists who are particularly sensitive to the atmosphere of its rural setting.

Near the cliff, the **church** in the middle of the graveyard, has one stained glass window by Ubac and another by Braque, who is buried beside the dramatist Porto Riche and the musician A. Roussel ; his grave faces seawards. A series of stained glass windows by Braque is to be found in **Saint Dominic's Chapel.**

From **Ailly Lighthouse,** there is a panoramic view over the surrounding countryside. An insect-eating plant grows in this area. It is known locally as "rossolis" and is covered with a sticky substance.

In 1532, the rich Dieppe shipowner Jean Ango, maritime consultant to François I, built an elegant manor-house near Varengeville. A combination of brick and shale creates a red and black mosaic between the timbering, giving the walls an air of well-balanced austerity. **Ango's Manor,** a typical example of rural Renaissance architecture, was based to a large extent on Italian dwellings. The four wings of the building surround a central courtyard ; the façade on this side are highly-ornate and include a loggia with sculpted arches. This ornamentation is completed by geometric designs in relief and the skilful marquetry effect of the timbering and bonding which bring into play a range of subtle colours.

VERNEUIL-SUR-AVRE (Eure)
22 miles W. of Dreux.

Like Tillières and Nonancourt, the town of Verneuil was built in the 12th century by Henry I Beauclerk. It lies on the borders of the Ouche, Beauce and Perche regions. A castle was built on the site before the town came into being, for this is a strategic point on the R. Avre defending, as it does, the frontiers of France and Normandy. The so-called Fossés-le-Roi were filled with water from the R. Iton, which was diverted especially for the purpose ; the moats led to other fortified positions.

Verneuil was to undergo numerous attacks and was ignominiously captured during the One Hundred Years' War. In the town, which is dominated by the Madeleine Tower, there are some traces of the original fortifications, and a tall cylindrical keep called the **Grey Tower** (Tour Grise) which is built of hard limestone*. There are also picturesque old houses. The historian J. Carcopino was born in Verneuil.

Magdalen Church (église de la Madeleine), which has undergone much alteration work, is remarkable for the adjacent Flamboyant tower. It was built in the same period as the Butter Tower in Rouen (late 15th — early 16th century). It was the gift of Arthus Fillon, a dignitary in the Ministry of Finance under François I. It is surmounted by a very ornate belfry and, on the piers, there is a series of sculptures by local craftsmen. Inside the church, the most noteworthy elements in its decoration are the 15th and 16th century 'pictorial' stained glass, a 15th century statue of the Virgin Mary holding an apple, and a monument to the Royalist rebel Louis de Frotté by David d'Angers.

In **Notre Dame Church,** which was built of hard limestone*, and which has been the subject of much restoration work, a moving and somewhat naive set of statues made by local artists in the early 16th century line the walls.

The Le Veneur family once occupied the castle (now almost completely ruined) in **Tillières-sur-Avre.** This village was the first settlement ever built to defend the 'Avre Line' and, during the Renaissance, the family donated money to the church for the building of its very ornate rib vaulting.

The Gothic church in the village of **Nonancourt** has 16th century stained glass windows.

VERNIER MARSHES — PONT AUDEMER (Eure)
22 miles N.E. of Lisieux.

Surrounded by a semi-circle of wooded hills on the edge of the Roumois Plateau, the former arm of the sea that is now the **Vernier Marshes** forms a vast alluvial plain (covering 19 sq. miles) reclaimed from the Seine Estuary after large-scale drainage projects. In or about 1607, Henri IV ordered the construction of the 'Dutchmen's Dike' by pioneers from the North. Since 1950, canals have helped to dry out the marshland, which now consists of grazing land, allotments and a wildfowl reserve. The water flows into the Grande Mare and is directed to the R. Seine by way of the Saint Aubin Canal.

La Roque Lighthouse serves as a lookout post for the entire estuary. A narrow channel has been dredged through the estuary, and river pilots do a vital job in guiding shipping through it. The earliest river pilots on the Seine worked from **Quillebœuf** in the 14th century ; it was reputed to be a very dangerous passage because of the tidal bore (a phenomenon which has now almost disappeared : see Caudebec). During the French Revolution, a ship carrying the Crown Jewels is said to have sunk at this particular spot. Nowadays, there are approximately 160 river pilots taking shipping up and down the Seine.

On the lower reaches of the R. Risle, the old tanning town of **Pont-Audemer** is rather unusual, with its canals and old houses. In the chapels leading off the side-aisles in **Saint Ouen's Church,** there are Renaissance stained glass windows depicting the lives of Saint Ouen and Saint Nicholas.

The **Roumois Plateau** is bordered to the north by the Seine Estuary, the Vernier Marshes and the Brotonne Forest, and flanked by the rivers Risle and Seine. To the south, it spreads out between the Montfort, La Lande and Elbeuf Forests until it joins the Neubourg Plateau. This a traditional belt where mixed farming is the main activity, but it has nevertheless been affected by the economic expansion and growing population of the neighbouring areas : there is some movement away from the rural areas towards the towns.

VERNON (Eure)
20 miles N.E. of Evreux.

Situated opposite chalk cliffs on the left bank of the Seine near the Bizy Forest, the mediaeval town of Vernon was established in the 10th century at the gateway to Normandy by the first Duke, Rollo. Several half-timbered houses survived the bombardments of 1944 which destroyed the 12th century **bridge.** Its ruins can be seen from the new bridge, as can the remains of **Tourelles Castle** on the right bank.

Building work on **Notre Dame Collegiate Church,** which was begun in the 11th century, continued throughout the entire Gothic period with corresponding variations in style. Above a 15th century portal, a Flamboyant rose window is flanked by slender turrets connected by a gallery. At the end of the nave, which is taller than the chancel, is a Renaissance organ loft. Stained glass from the same period and 17th century tapestries decorate the interior.

From **Saint Michael's Hill** (côte Saint-Michel), on the right bank of the river, the visitor can look down over the R. Seine and the town.

Bizy Castle (18th century) with its oubuildings and stables laid out in an orderly Classical fashion reminiscent of Versailles, once belonged to Louis-Philippe who restored the park. The main part of the building was rebuilt during the Second Empire in the Italian style. The Baroque gardens have been relandscaped.

VILLEDIEU-LES-POELES (Manche)
22 miles S. of Saint-Lô.

Near the zooligical garden of Champrepus in the Bocage Region, the small town of Villedieu-les-Poëles with its picturesque streams and old houses has been the home of coppersmiths since the Middle Ages. What was once a cottage industry with an output of church ornaments and kitchenware, has been given over to mass-production and has been diversified to include less functional items. The industry's history is depicted at the **Pots and Pans Museum** (Musée de la Poeslerie).

Another noble tradition, that of the bell-foundry, has been maintained in the town since the 12th century when the Knights of Malta, the Order founded by Henry I Beauclerk, brought back the secret of bronze alloys from the East (the Grand Consecration ceremony is still held every four years). The **Cornille-Havard Foundry** is open to the public.

VILLEQUIER (Seine-Maritime)
25 miles W. of Rouen.

On 4th September 1843, during a boat trip on the R. Seine, the beloved daughter of Victor Hugo, Léopoldine, was drowned with her young husband, Charles Vacquerie, and two close relatives, when the tidal bore swept them overboard (cf. Caudebec). The dramatic accident, which was to mark the poet for the rest of his life, is recalled in the **Victor Hugo Museum** housed in the Vacquerie's old home where memorabilia of the writer and his family are on show. Madame Hugo is buried in the village cemetery, next to the victims of the accident.

VIRE (Calvados)
25 miles S.E. of Saint-Lô.

This small town is the capital of the hilly Bocage Virois Region and a centre of the dairy industry and cattle-breeding. It is set in such picturesque surroundings that it had to be fortified against attack very early in its history.

Although damaged after the Normandy Landings of 1944, it still has a **Clock Gate** (Porte-Horloge) with a belfry (1480) that dominates the main square, and several towers. The remains of the Romanesque keep, built by Henry I Beauclerk at the top of an outcrop of rock, look down over the **Vire Valleys,** narrow passes where cotton was once fulled. It is said that the term 'vaudeville' comes from 'vaudevires', the jovial songs performed by one Olivier Basselin, a journeyman fuller of the 15th century. As to Vire chitterlings, their reputation was made long ago.

On the Saint-Lô road, is the 16th century castle of **Torigni-sur-Vire,** the fief of the Matignon family. It has been restored.

The picturesque rough Vire Valley has been carved out of old schist. From the **Ham Rocks,** there is a view across a deep bend of the river.

The well-proportioned granite **minster** of **Saint-Sever-Calvados** (13th-14th century) was once part of a monastery founded by a future bishop of Avranches, Sever, and later given to the Benedictine Order. Nearby is state-owned **Saint Sever's Forest.**

YVETOT (Seine-Maritime)
22 miles N.W. of Rouen.

This large prosperous market town in the heart of the Caux Region was damaged in the last war. From 1392 to 1551, the lords of the manor had the singular habit of giving themselves the title of 'King' — hence the famous song by Béranger.

In **Saint Peter's Church** (église Saint-Pierre), a modern circular place of worship, huge stained glass windows by Max Ingrand depict the lives of the Norman saints.

A few miles away is one of the oldest trees in France, the one-thousand-year-old **Allouville Oak.** Chapels have been cut into its trunk which measures 48 ft. in circumference.

GLOSSARY

Arching : Concentric arches above a bay.

Barbican : A forework ensuring the external defences of a fortress.

Barrel-vaulting : Hemicylindrical vaulting.

Bonding : The method of cutting and assembling brick or stone in buildings.

Coffers : Hollow panels decorated with moulding or art work that ornament ceilings or vaulted roofs.

Corner-stone : A flat triangular surface between two adjacent arches.

Curtain-wall : A rampart between two bastions or two towers.

Foliage : A sculpted or painted ornamentation that consists of leaves forming volutes.

Gable : A triangular pediment (often decorated) at the top of a wall, or above a door or a window.

Hard limestone : A natural ferruginous conglomerate.

Lancets : The elongated painted arches characteristic of the 13th century Gothic style.

Leaf : The section of a door or gate which opens.

Misericords : Brackets (often carved) beneath choirstalls.

Motte : A manmade mound or hillock.

Peristyle : A row of columns standing out from the façade of a building.

Pinnacle : A slender structure surmounting a pier or a pediment (it increases the stability of the building).

Postern-gate : A door hidden in ramparts, leading to the moat.

Squinch : A small triangular arch designed to facilitate a change in architectural form from square to octogonal (e.g. in the building of a dome), or to support any overhanging part of a building.

Triforium : A narrow row of arches above the side-aisles opening onto the nave of a church.

Weather-boarding : Short, thin boards supporting tiles or slates on a roof or covering the outside walls of a building.

BIBLIOGRAPHY

BELY L. — **Les Abbayes normandes,** Rennes, Ouest-France 1979.

BELY L. — **Le Mont Saint-Michel,** Rennes, Ouest-France 1979.

BELY L. — **Art roman en Normandie,** Rennes, Ouest-France 1980.

BERTRAND S. — **La Tapisserie de Bayeux,** Rennes, Ouest-France 1977.

BOUARD M. de — **Histoire de la Normandie,** Toulouse, Privat 1975.

BRUNET P. — **Villes et villages de Normandie,** Wettolsheim, Ed. Mars et Mercure 1978.

CAMBY P. — **Bagnoles-de-l'Orne,** Rennes, Ouest-France 1980.

CARTON J. — **Le Mont Saint-Michel,** Paris, Arthaud 1949.

COMPAGNON Général J. — **Les Plages du Débarquement,** Rennes, Ouest-France 1979.

DECAENS H. — **Rouen,** Rennes, Ouest-France 1980.

DELALONDE M. — **Manuscrits du Mont Saint-Michel,** Rennes, Ouest-France 1981.

DUMESNIL R. — **Au fil de la Seine, de Paris à la mer** (Visages du monde), Paris, Horizons de France 1960.

DUNCOMBE F. — **Caen,** Rennes, Ouest-France 1977.

FAVIER J. — **La Normandie racontée aux enfants,** Rennes, Ouest-France 1978.

FREGNAC C. — **Merveilles des châteaux de Normandie,** Paris, Hachette-Réalités 1966.

HERUBEL M. — **Contes populaires de toutes les Normandie,** Rennes, Ouest-France 1978.

Guide Bleu Hachette, **Normandie.**

Guide Vert Michelin, **Normandie.**

Guide Seuil, **Seine-Maritime.**

HERVAL R. — **En Normandie,** Paris, Arthaud 1971.

HUREAU J. — **La Normandie aujourd'hui,** Paris, Jeune Afrique 1981.

LACOTTE D. — **Les Châteaux du Cotentin,** Rennes, Ouest-France 1979.

LELIEVRE R. — **Vieilles demeures, manoirs et châteaux normands,** Coutances, Ed. N.D. 1966.

LE POVREMOYNE J. — **La Normandie** (Voir en couleurs), Paris, Delpire 1965.

PILLEMENT G. — **La France inconnue, Nord et Normandie,** Paris, Grasset 1959.

POPOVITCH O. — **La Faïence de Rouen,** Rennes, Ouest-France 1979.

Revue des Monuments Historiques, n° 103, **Les Abbayes normandes,** juin 1979.

Revue "Nouvelles de l'Eure", quelques numéros anciens.

ROMAN J. — **Toute la Normandie,** 1965.

SCHNERB F. — **Honfleur,** Rennes, Ouest-France 1978.

SCHNERB F. — **Pont-l'Evêque,** Rennes, Ouest-France 1977.

TARTINVILLE P. et Y. **Les Châteaux normands,** Rennes, Ouest-France 1981.

INDEX

PHOTOGRAPHS TAKEN BY

Daniel Gréard : pages 2-3, 116.

Jean-Paul Gisserot : pages, 6, 10-11, 14, 15, 19, 22, 27, 41, 53, 56, 57, 61, 66-67, 70-71, 75, 82, 83, 86, 90-91, 100, 101, 104, 105, 108, 113, 117, 121, 124, 128, front and back covers.

Ville de Bayeux : pages 7, 48-49.

Hervé Champollion : 18, 79, 94, 109, 112, 125.

Frank Duncombe : pages 23, 27, 33, 60, 78.

Dominique Le Tellier : 26, 40, 52.

Guy Desmesne - Yves Tartinville : 30-31, 44-45, 95, 120.

Nicolas Fediaevsky : 36-37, 64.

Alain Le Berre : 74.

Olivier Schnerb : 87, 97.